THE DRAGON IN THE ROOM

THE DRAGON IN
THE ROOM

China and the

Future of Latin

American

Industrialization

**Kevin P. Gallagher and
Roberto Porzecanski**

STANFORD UNIVERSITY PRESS
Stanford, California

Stanford University Press
Stanford, California

Special discounts for bulk quantities of Stanford Business Books are available to
corporations, professional associations, and other organizations. For details and
discount information, contact the special sales department of Stanford University
Press. Tel: (650) 736-1782, Fax: (650) 736-1784

Printed in the United States of America on acid-free, archival-quality paper

Library of Congress Cataloging-in-Publication Data
Gallagher, Kevin, 1968–
    The dragon in the room : China and the future of Latin American
industrialization / Kevin P. Gallagher and Roberto Porzecanski.
        p. cm.
    Includes bibliographical references and index.
    ISBN 978-0-8047-7187-0 (cloth : alk. paper)—ISBN 978-0-8047-7188-7
(pbk. : alk. paper) 1. Latin America—Commerce—China. 2. China—
Commerce—Latin America. 3. Exports—Latin America. 4. Exports—
China. 5. Industrialization—Latin America. I. Porzecanski, Roberto. II. Title.
    HF3230.5.Z7G35 2010
    338.098—dc22
                                                                    2010018618

Typeset by Westchester Book Services in 10/13.5pt Sabon

Contents

List of Figures

List of Tables

Preface and Acknowledgments

In the earlier part of the decade, Kevin P. Gallagher and colleague Lyuba Zarsky were spending a significant amount of time in Mexico conducting research on the extent to which foreign investment into Mexico's high-technology sector produced broad benefits for the Mexican economy under the North American Free Trade Agreement (NAFTA). In the early years of our research, most of the business leaders we talked to were very optimistic about their future as key exporters to the United States. Indeed, they saw such exports as an engine that could upgrade Mexico's manufacturing capabilities and eventually move the nation away from being a low-skilled assembly manufacturer. Later in the decade all anyone in Mexican manufacturing wanted to talk about was China. We went on to publish our work in a book titled *The Enclave Economy: Foreign Investment and Sustainable Development in Mexico's Silicon Valley*.

The United Nations Economic Commission for Latin America (ECLAC) also shared concern about China. In 2004, ECLAC's research director in Mexico, Juan Carlos Moreno Brid, and Kevin Gallagher decided to conduct a comprehensive assessment of the competitiveness of Mexican exports vis-à-vis China. They teamed with Uruguayan political economist Roberto Porzecanski to write an article on the subject, which appeared in the journal *World Development*. Chapter 5 of this book draws heavily from that early work.

While Juan Carlos went on to write his comprehensive book on the Mexican economy with Jaime Ros, titled *Development and Growth in the Mexican Economy*, Roberto and Kevin continued to delve deeper into the China–Latin America economic relationship. More than five years later, the result of that effort is this book.

We are grateful to the many people and organizations that made this book possible. First we want to thank the Global Development and Environment Institute (GDAE) at Tufts University. At GDAE we would specifically like to thank Tim Wise, GDAE's research director, for guidance and support. Wise and GDAE's Ann Helwege provided friendly but sharp comments and backing throughout the process. Our colleagues Neva Goodwin, Jonathan Harris, and Brian Roach provided valuable feedback during GDAE seminars where we first shared our preliminary findings. Frank Ackerman of the Stockholm Environment Institute works out of the GDAE offices and provided numerous insights as well. Last but not least, we would like to thank Joshua Berkowitz, Lauren Denizard, and Mukhtar Amin for providing cheerful and important administrative support throughout the process.

In addition to the early paper in *World Development*, very preliminary versions of some of these chapters appeared as working papers at the University of California–Berkeley's Center for Latin American Studies and at the University of Massachusetts–Amherst's Political Economy Research Institute. We thank Harley Shaiken at Berkeley and Gerald Epstein at UMass for giving us these venues to get early feedback on our preliminary findings. Chapter 6 draws heavily on a working paper written by Kevin Gallagher with Mehdi Shafaeddin for the IDEAS network. We thank Mehdi for a wonderful collaboration and International Development Economics Associates (IDEAS)for allowing us to get early feedback on that preliminary work as well.

We also had numerous opportunities to present versions of these chapters at conferences and workshops over the past five years. We thank the David Rockefeller Center for Latin American Studies at Harvard University, Mt. Holyoke College, Connecticut College, and Rensselaer Polytechnic Institute for inviting one of us to present this work in seminar form. We also presented parts of this work at numerous conferences convened by the New England Council for Latin American Studies, the Latin

American Studies Association, and the Society for the Advancement of Socio-Economics.

We are grateful for financial support from the Ford Foundation, the Rockefeller Brothers Fund, General Services Foundation, and Boston University for funding us to conduct this research.

Boston University continues to provide a great home to Kevin Gallagher. He thanks his students and colleagues for continued inspiration and ideas. Gallagher also sincerely thanks the Frederick S. Pardee Center for the Study of the Longer-Range Future for making him a faculty fellow and supporting some of the research for this volume.

We thank Stacy Wagner and Stanford University Press for their faith in this book. We also thank Jessica Walsh, Puja Sangar, and Kate Wahl at SUP.

We also just have to thank the staff and ownership at Anna's Taqueria in Davis Square for the delicious meals that provided the energy for a big part of our project, as well as for the environment in which many critical discussions about this book took place. We will have to walk from lecture to lecture on our book tour to burn off all those wonderful calories!

We dedicate this volume to our loving and supportive families. Kevin thanks his wife, Kelly, and children, Theodore and Estelle, for their never-ending love, cheer, and support. Roberto thanks his parents, Ignacio and Martha, his sisters, Ana Luz and Isabel, and his grandmother, Linda, for their unconditional love and support. He especially thanks Karen, his wife, for being his source of inspiration, for her precious love, and for the invaluable encouragement and support she provided throughout this and all other endeavors in the last twelve years.

THE DRAGON IN THE ROOM

1 Enter the Dragon

"China is an awakening monster that can eat us."
Carlos Zúñiga, Nicaraguan CAFTA negotiator
La Prensa *(Nicaragua), March 10, 2004*

"What are the factors driving the crisis of the textile sector? First is the global competition of China, which is more and more present in every market."
Isaac Soloducho, president of Paylana, a leading exporter of high-quality wool-based apparel in Uruguay
El Observador *(Uruguay), November 20, 2006, p.13*

There is a growing clamor in Latin America and the Caribbean (LAC) over the extent to which the region is being economically swallowed by China. Some claim that China's exports are flooding domestic LAC markets and wiping out local firms. Others refer to China as an "angel" for the region that will deliver the fruits of growth by importing LAC goods and investing in the LAC region. Yet there is no contention at all in LAC (or anywhere else) that China's export-led economic expansion since the early 1980s has been anything short of a miracle.

Amid all this chatter, what is strikingly absent from the discussion is a clear understanding of how China is globalizing its economy and what lessons that method might lend to the conundrum of economic development in LAC. Yes, China's growing appetite for primary products, and the ability of Latin America to supply that demand, played a role in restoring growth in Latin America, both in the run-up to the global financial crisis and in its aftermath. Yet, the dragon in the room that few are talking about is that China is simultaneously out-competing Latin American manufactures in world markets—so much so that it may threaten the ability of the region to generate long-run economic growth. What receives even less attention is that China's road to globalization, one that emphasizes gradualism and coordinated macro-economic and industrial policies, is far superior to the "Washington Consensus" route taken by most Latin American nations, particularly Mexico. And if LAC does not change its development strategy, many of the region's deepest fears could come home to roost. China may not be the problem, LAC's policies may be. China's rise may be able to offer clues for a better path.

This book is an attempt to confront these conversations head-on. We conduct a thorough analysis of China's economic relationship with LAC as well as an analysis of China's trade-led industrialization strategy.[1]

Specifically, we ask the question "To what extent has China's rising economic expansion benefited LAC countries?" We answer this question by looking at the bilateral trade that has blossomed between China and LAC in recent years. We also examine the competitiveness of LAC manufactures exports in world and regional markets relative to China. This exercise leads us to four central findings.

- LAC exports to China are heavily concentrated in a handful of countries and sectors, leaving the majority of LAC without the opportunity to significantly gain from China as a market for their exports.
- China is increasingly outcompeting LAC manufactures exports in world and regional markets, and the worst may be yet to come.
- China is rapidly building the technological capabilities necessary for industrial development, whereas LAC is not paying enough attention to innovation and industrial development.
- These three trends could accentuate a pattern of specialization in LAC that will hurt LAC's longer run prospects for economic development.

Our findings, which confirm and expand upon most of the recent peer-reviewed literature, imply that neither a hysterical fear of China nor optimistic complacency have much justification across the region. What is more, when one confronts the dragon in the room, we learn that China's rise is both a warning sign and an opportunity for LAC. China's rise is the latest warning to LAC that it cannot sit back with a laissez-faire attitude about economic policy and hope that such an attitude will automatically translate into growth and prosperity. China's rise is an opportunity because China's direct and indirect impacts on LAC exports will allow a handful of countries in the region to build reserves and bolster the region's fiscal position, enabling LAC to rekindle a serious discussion about industrial development for the twenty-first century.

Two Globalizations

Development derives from a process of diversifying an economy from concentrated assets based on primary products to a diverse set of assets based on knowledge. This process involves investing in human, physical and natural capital in manufacturing, and services (Amsden 2001, 2–3). Imbs and Wacziarg (2003) have confirmed that nations that develop follow this trajectory. They find that as nations get richer, sectoral production and employment move from a relatively high concentration to diversity. They find that nations do not stabilize their diversity until their populations reach a mean annual income of over $15,000. The question for development and trade policy then becomes "What policies will help facilitate the diversification and development process without conflicting with trade rules or jeopardizing the needs of future generations?"

The answer to this question will differ across the developing world depending on the particular binding constraints that a country's growth trajectory faces. The development policies for a small, vulnerable nation such as Haiti will be significantly different from countries like Brazil, India, and China, which may be looking to diversify beyond primary products and light manufacturing to high-tech manufacturing and services-based economic growth that develops endogenous productive capacity. Recent work in development economics shows that nations need to engage in a process of "self-discovery" whereby they undergo a diagnosis of what the binding constraints to economic growth may be (Rodrik 2007).

To some extent, China and LAC went through a diagnostic period just over thirty years ago. After such a process, both China and most of the countries in LAC determined that one of the binding constraints on their economic development was a lack of appreciation for markets in general and the world economy in particular. Although LAC is, of course, capitalist and China has remained socialist at least on paper, LAC and China have had similar goals over the past thirty years. Thirty years ago, both China and LAC were largely practicing a government-led economic policy that shied away from the world economy. In both China and LAC there were signs that such an approach had run its course. As we show in greater detail in Chapter 6, both China and LAC sought to reform themselves by embracing markets in general and the world economy in particular. In 1978 for China, and 1982 for LAC, both places began to dismantle many of the vestiges of their old economic ways in favor of exports, foreign direct investment, and freer markets.

That is where the similarities end, however. LAC's approach to globalization has infamously been referred to as the embrace of the "Washington Consensus"—the fairly rapid liberalization of trade and investment regimes and the general decrease of the role of the state in economic affairs. Beginning in the early 1990s, LAC nations began to rapidly dismantle the role of the state in economic affairs. Although, of course, there are significant differences between countries, generally speaking LAC unilaterally privatized the majority of its state-owned enterprises, liberalized trade and investment, and limited government activity in macroeconomic policy, then locked in these reforms through joining the World Trade Organization (WTO). Some countries went even further in locking in these reforms by adopting the disciplines contained in free-trade agreements with the United States and other developed countries.

As we detail in Chapter 6, China's approach to globalization could not be more different. In contrast to the "shock therapy" practiced in LAC, China has globalized by what Deng Xiaoping said was "crossing the river by feeling each stone." China's more gradual and experimental approach to reform allowed for the development of domestic firms and industries before liberalizing fully. More importantly, it also created an environment so that the potential "losers" from liberalization would be less numerous. Finally, China has shied away from trade deals with the United States and has focused more on the more multilateral WTO, which it joined in 2001. The results, shown in table 1.1, are stark.

Table 1.1 covers the period 1960 to 2007. For LAC the "pre-reform period" runs from 1960 to 1982, for China from 1960 to 1978. LAC started out with a higher GDP, a higher level of income, fewer people in poverty, and higher levels of trade and investment. And in terms of growth in income, LAC as a whole still remains much richer than China. Yet what jumps out in this table is that LAC has barely gained ground during its reform period, and China has excelled.

TABLE 1.1   China and LAC in Comparative Perspective, 1960 to 2007

	Pre-reform		Post-reform	
	LAC	China	LAC	China
Growth				
GDP, PPP* (trillions of constant 2005 int'l $)	2.7	0.53	3.6	2.6
GDP growth (% annual)	2.7	4.8	2.6	9.9
Manufacturing growth (% annual)	4.2	10.8	2.2	11.5
Income and Poverty				
GDP per capita, PPP (constant 2005 int'l $)	7,413	533	7,665	2,068
GDP per capita growth (% annual)	2.7	3.4	1.0	9.0
Poverty head-count ratio at $1.25 a day (PPP) (% of population)	12.9	84.0	11.4	44.2
Trade and Investment				
Trade (% of GDP)	22.0	11.8	35.9	42.2
Foreign direct investment, net inflows (% of GDP)	0.8	0.1	2.0	2.7
Gross capital formation (% of GDP)	22.0	26.5	20.1	38.8

SOURCE: Authors' calculations based on World Bank (2009).
*NOTE: GDP=gross domestic product; PPP=Purchasing Power Parity.

By every measure China has outreformed and outperformed LAC. Whereas LAC's GDP growth since reforms has been 2.6 percent annually and only 1 percent in per capita terms, China's growth has been an unprecedented 9.9 and 9 percent respectively. Whereas LAC still has many fewer people in poverty than China does, China has decreased the number of people in poverty (in the order of hundreds of millions) by half, and LAC by just over 10 percent, one percentage point. And when it comes to indicators of globalization itself—trade and investment—China trades more and outperforms in terms of investment.

All is not rosy in China, however. The environmental costs of China's growth miracle are of grave concern. China has become the world's largest emitter of carbon dioxide, and it is also riddled with contaminated water supplies and localized air pollution (Economy 2004). In addition, inequality has become a concern on China's booming eastern coast.

Of course, LAC does not need to compare itself to China. In many ways, when China reformed, it was starting out much further behind than LAC. What matters most is how LAC is faring in general. Looked at on its own, LAC growth is lackluster but not terrible. In contrast with sub-Saharan Africa and parts of South Asia, growth has been positive, and, with the exception of the years during financial crises, poverty has not increased.

What does call for attention, however, is the extent to which China affects LAC's longer-term prospects for development. Will China's extraordinary growth spill over to LAC, or will China attract investment and trade that will divert from LAC? These are the questions we dwell on in this book.

Book Overview

This book examines the extent to which China's rising economic expansion has benefited or damaged LAC countries and draws implications for the future. We take an empirically based approach to this question from a number of angles. Throughout this volume we analyze the bilateral trade relationship between China and LAC countries, and the extent to which China and LAC compete in world markets. We want this work to be accessible to policymakers, students, and academics outside the economics profession, as well as to economists. For that reason, we have transferred the details of our methodological approach to a technical appendix in the back of the book so that the reader can get a crisp and clear understanding of our findings and their implications. Aside from the appendices, the volume has six chapters. Even with the appendices in the book, the reader may find some parts of the chapters to be fairly dense. Given how underresearched this area is to date, we make scores of calculations to answer our research questions. We have streamlined them to the extent we could, but discussion of the most important calculations is unavoidable. Taken together, this effort tells a story that is important for researchers and policymakers to understand. That said, this first chapter very briefly introduces and outlines our research and findings and puts them in context.

Chapter 2 performs a detailed analysis of the bilateral trade and investment relationship between LAC and China. In this chapter we calculate the levels of China–LAC trade. We find that China has had a positive impact on LAC through this channel in two ways. First, China's rise has led to an increase in demand for LAC products. Since 2000 China's imports from LAC have quintupled, reaching close to $25 billion in 2006. More indirectly, China's economic expansion and corresponding demand have increased the prices of many of the goods that LAC trades, and therefore LAC improved its terms of trade in part owing to China (at least until 2007). Finally, the increase in trade directly and indirectly caused by China has given LAC more reserves that can prove useful during an economic crisis such as the current one.

The China boom has not been without cost for LAC, however. Although the level of LAC exports to China has surged of late, exports to China as a share of total LAC exports have stayed the same for decades. What is more, six countries and ten commodities dominate all LAC trade with China, meaning that many LAC countries have not seen much of a change in exports at all as a result of China. Of more concern is that virtually all of LAC's exports to China are in the form of primary commodities. Commodities markets are notoriously volatile, and the long-term trend for commodities prices is negative. If China demand then contributes to an increase in the specialization of LAC production, LAC's terms of trade could deteriorate and affect the region's growth prospects for decades. Moreover, without the proper environmental policies in place, surges in commodities exports to China can leave a large environmental footprint. Many of these potential costs can be avoided if some of the potential benefits of China trade are set aside to mitigate those costs.

The costs of lost world market need to be juxtaposed alongside the benefits of increased exports to China. In Chapter 3 we examine the extent to which LAC is competing with China in world and regional manufacturing markets. Based on measures of export similarity and initial market share, only a handful of countries compete with China (at present): Argentina, Brazil, Chile, Colombia, Costa Rica, and Mexico. We calculate the extent to which manufactures exports in these and other LAC countries are "threatened"—meaning that China's growth in an export sector is much faster than a LAC competitor in that sector—by China's rise. Astonishingly, we find that 94 percent of LAC's manufactures are threatened by China, representing 40 percent of all LAC exports. LAC manufactures are still growing, but at a slower pace and in sectors where China is rapidly increasing its market share.

The jewel of manufactures trade, and trade-led growth in general, is high technology. Nations that diversify into high-technology exports grow faster and better. Some LAC nations, particularly Argentina, Brazil, and Mexico, made significant inroads in global high-tech markets during the high-tech boom of the 1990s. Chapter 4 focuses on the extent to which China is outcompeting LAC high-technology manufacturing and services exports in world and regional markets. China's rise in this regard has been unprecedented. We find that China has gone from being one of the most insignificant high-technology exporters to the number-one high-technology manufacturer in the world. The only two LAC nations that have maintained some significance in international competitiveness are Brazil and Mexico. We find that 95 percent of all high-technology exports in LAC are under some threat from China. What is additionally striking about the Chinese case is that China's composition of high-technology exports has not only increased but also diversified during its surge. In other words, whereas China started its high-tech export surge by serving as a low-wage haven for low-skilled goods, it has climbed the technology ladder and now exports personal computers, cars, appliances, and other high-tech goods under Chinese name brands. Mexico, on the other hand, has gained competitiveness only in low-wage, low-skilled high-tech goods.

Because Mexico tops everyone's list of nations under direct threat from China, we devote two whole chapters to the Mexican case. Chapter 5 empirically examines the extent to which China is outcompeting Mexico in Mexico's most important external market, the United States. By any measure and in every analysis, Mexico stands out as the most similar to China (in terms of export structure) and mostly likely to be affected by it in world markets. In Chapter 5, then, we perform a Mexico-specific analysis and confirm that Mexico is already experiencing cutthroat competition with China that is starting to have a very negative effect. Ninety-nine percent of Mexico's manufactures exports, comprising 72 percent of all Mexican exports, are under threat from China. As we show in this chapter, many manufacturing firms have relocated from Mexico to China, and statistical analyses show that China is significantly affecting Mexican manufacturing in a negative manner.

Chapter 6 tries to shed some light on the causes of China's relative increase in competitiveness, going behind the statistical analyses of previous chapters and conducting a comparative analysis of trade and industrial reform in China and Mexico, the LAC country most affected by China. It is striking how two countries with very similar profiles of manufacturing exports that liberalized both their markets ended up on very different trajectories. Based on field research, statistical analysis, and an assessment of the peer-reviewed literature, we detail macroeconomic, trade, and industrial innovation policy in the two countries during the period of reform. What becomes clear is that China has actively managed the globalization process, and Mexico thought that markets alone could manage Mexico's economy.

In Chapter 7 we summarize our results and key findings and draw implications for research and policy. Rather than blaming China for LAC's poor performance, we encourage the LAC region to look inward for the source of its lack of competitiveness and slippage into a dangerous trend toward relying solely on primary commodities. This is a trend that plagued the region in the nineteenth century, and no one wants to go back to it. Indeed, China's example may be the real lesson of the past thirty years. In no way do we surmise that LAC should go back to the (albeit high-growth) policies it deployed between 1940 and 1970. Trade, foreign investment, and embracing global markets will clearly be an important part of any economic strategy in the twenty-first century. However, what is clear from China's case is that it has had a more successful approach to economic reform and globalization.

At the very least, the findings in this book should spark a pragmatic discussion of the role of technology and industry in twenty-first-century economic development. Twentieth-century LAC was plagued by extremes in terms of economic policy. During the early part of the century, LAC engaged in heavy-handed economic policy that had some gains but eventually ran its course. The latter part of the century was characterized by a complete pendulum swing to what one might call free-market fundamentalism. Though not without its successes as well, the Washington Consensus has largely failed in LAC. What is needed is a pragmatic approach that must include a discussion of the role of technology, innovation, and industry. Economic theory tells us that nations with a more diversified economy grow faster and are more stable. LAC is going in the opposite direction, in part magnified by China's rise. It is time for policy-makers and business people to forge a balanced approach to economic development whereby the state helps to foster an environment where the private market can thrive and compete. LAC is promising because it still has a considerable manufacturing base from which it can build. Thanks in part to China, it also is in a better fiscal and monetary position than since before the 1980s. LAC stands with an opportunity to put its development problems behind it in the twenty-first century, but such an opportunity will not be seized automatically.

2   China to the Rescue?

*China and the Latin American
Commodities Boom*

Before the financial crisis of 2008, many analysts argued that China's rapid growth was a savior for LAC economic development. China's rise, they said, led to an increase in demand for LAC commodities exports and a general increase in the prices for those exports across the world. What's more, in the postcrisis period, many in the region hope that China can help pull LAC out of its worst recession in a decade by the same means.

This book in general, and this chapter in particular, sheds a critical light on these claims. In this chapter we find that China's impact on Latin American commodities exports has been highly concentrated in a few countries and sectors. Throughout the rest of the book, we show that China is indeed outcompeting LAC manufactures exports across the globe. And China's efforts in a post-crisis world may solidify these trends.

Indeed, if these trends persist, China may be playing a role in putting Latin America back into a world of primary product dependency and fiercely outperforming Latin America in global manufacturing markets. As we argue in the first chapter, China's growth is indeed a very positive achievement—most of all because China is home to the highest number of people in the world living on less than $2.50 per day. However, China's impact on LAC exports and the prices of some key products has been relatively small. Therefore, we argue in this chapter that the longer-term implications may not be such a cause for optimism. For LAC, the best thing about China's growth may be lessons that can be drawn in terms of a more comprehensive development strategy for the region.

More specifically, in this chapter we analyze the extent to which Chinese demand is enhancing the performance of Latin American economies. First, we calculate the growth in LAC exports in recent years. To approximate the extent to which China demand has propelled such exports, we then calculate the share of global export growth in those LAC export-growth sectors that can be attributed to China. We then examine bilateral trade with China, analyzing the total amount and sectoral composition of such trade, and the major countries involved in China LAC trade. We find that China is having a direct and indirect impact on LAC exports, but an impact limited to only a handful of countries in certain sectors.

This chapter has five key findings:

- **China matters:** China is responsible for a growing part of global demand and is somewhat affecting price increases in and exports from LAC; yet,
- **LAC's exports to China are a small percentage:** Exports to China were only 3.8 percent of all LAC exports. In other words, 96.2 percent of all LAC exports do not go to China. Moreover, growth in LAC exports to China was only 8 percent of all LAC export growth since the boom began in 2000;
- **China's imports from LAC are a small percentage:** LAC's exports to China comprised only 5.8 percent of Chinese imports, the same level of LAC exports to China in the 1980s;
- **Beneficiaries of LAC–China trade are concentrated:** Ten sectors in six countries account for 74 percent of all LAC exports to China and 91 percent of all LAC commodities exports to China;
- **LAC is a primary-product exporter to China:** 74 percent of all LAC exports to China were in primary commodities.

The future does not look much better. Most of the projections about post-crisis trends in commodities prices show a return to the long-term trend of decreasing prices—though more booms (and more busts) seem to have become characteristic of these markets for the twenty-first century. When booms do occur it is not clear that LAC nations have the proper countercyclical policies in place to benefit from them. As we show in this chapter, Chile and a handful of other countries have stabilization funds thatshould be effective in the wake of the current crisis. However, even Chile—as we will see, the poster child of Latin American sound macroeconomic management—falls short in terms of steering such funds into diversification.

In sum, we find that China is having a relatively small impact on the region except in a handful of countries and sectors. Moreover, as of 2009 and in the wake of the financial and economic crisis that started in 2008, the prices in most of those sectors have already begun to drop quite dramatically. We find little concrete evidence for a resource curse, though this needs to be studied in more depth. We also find that, contrary to past booms, some countries in LAC have the mechanisms in place to transfer some of the rents from the recent boom toward long-run development.

Ride the China Train

In a special report devoted to "China's Thirst for Resources," the *Economist* magazine argued that China's growth provides an unparalleled opportunity for Latin America (and Africa) and captured the optimism that existed before the outset of the crisis:

> African and Latin American economies are growing at their fastest pace in decades, thanks in large part to heavy Chinese demand for their resources. China's burgeoning consumption has helped push the price of all manner of fuels, metals and grains to new peaks over the past year. Even the price of shipping raw materials recently reached a record. Analysts see little prospect of an end to the boom; the prices of a few commodities have fallen on the back of America's worsening economic outlook, but others, including oil, wheat and iron ore, continue to set new records. China, with about a fifth of the world's population, now consumes half of its cement, a third of its steel and over a quarter of its aluminum. Its imports of many natural resources are growing even faster than its bounding economy. Shipments of iron ore, for example, have risen by an average of 27% a year for the past four years. ("China's Thirst" 2008, 3)

The opportunities that China's rise presents have also been underscored by international institutions. Indeed, the most comprehensive assessments have been done by the World Bank, the Organization for Economic Cooperation and Development (OECD), and the Inter-American Development

Bank (IDB). These studies share the perspective that China's rise has been an important engine of Latin American growth.

The World Bank goes so far as to say that LAC "should be rooting for more growth," in China. The Bank goes on to add that "the rising correlation between the growth of the two Asian economies [China and India] and LAC economies (with the exception of Central America and the Caribbean) seems to have been mainly driven by demand externalities and higher prices for commodities where LAC's comparative advantage lies" (Lederman, Olarreaga, and Perry 2009, 7). Similarly, Blázquez-Lidoy, Rodríguez, and Santiso argue that "even when trade is concentrated in a small basket of commodities, China's strong demand for raw materials is good news for Latin America. In economic terms, this event could be considered as a positive demand shock. Even more, there is a positive impact on the region, even though direct trade with China does not rise" (2006, 26).

The Inter-American Development Bank shares this view:

> China's 1.3 billion people mean 1.3 billion potential consumers. Aggregate consumption in China is relatively low and bound to rise with growing levels of national income. Many Latin American countries are well positioned to supply the Chinese market with agricultural products, processed food, and beverages. For example, Argentina and Brazil have found an important market in China for their agro-food industries. As Chinese incomes grow, consumer tastes should also diversify, offering growth opportunities for exports such as wines, coffees, meats, fruits, and vegetables (some of which can exploit the inverted seasons of North-South temperate zones). China's expansion has fueled strong external demand for nonagricultural raw and processed materials as well. Latin American countries are exploiting this opportunity. For example, Chile has found an important market in China for copper, ores, wood, pulp, and slag and ash while Brazil is selling iron ore and pellets. (Devlin, Estevadeordal, and Rodriguez-Clare 2006)

The other side of the coin of these optimistic assessments regarding the positive impact of China's growth in Latin America has been a concern that China is accentuating LAC's dependence on primary commodities, which in turn could exacerbate long-held uneasiness in the region over commodity dependence (Phillips 2007). These concerns are rife throughout the literature. For example, the World Bank says:

The move towards natural-resource-intensive products implies a more concentrated export bundle in LAC. This raises concerns regarding the vulnerability of LAC to future (negative) terms of trade shocks, but more importantly there is also a feeling within LAC that the gains associated with natural-resource-intensive exports are not being widely spread. The economic, but also political, sustainability of this specialization in natural-resource-intensive sectors depends on the extent to which gains are shared with owners of other factors of production. (Devlin, Estevadeordal, and Rodriguez-Clare 2006)

This concern is also shared by Lall and Weiss, who argue:

LAC faces a more serious threat over the long term: the export specialization of most of LAC is heavily biased towards resource-based primary products, with a very small share of technology-intensive products. Chinese growth may thus constrain its ability to diversify into more dynamic and technologically advanced products, with potential harm to its dynamic comparative advantage. (Lall and Weiss 2005)

This chapter builds on this previous work by looking deeper at both the nature of LAC exports to China and the extent to which a possible shift toward primary and resource-based products is of concern to the region (González 2008).

China and the LAC Commodities Boom

Before the crisis, Latin American growth was being fueled by a commodities export boom. GDP in LAC has increased by almost 3.2 percent per annum for a total of 19 percent in real terms between 2000 and 2006. Much of that growth is explained by an export boom. Exports grew over 10 percent each year, and total export growth during the period was 62.5 percent. Between 2000 and 2006, 70 percent of the export growth in LAC was explained by the growth in the export of commodities.

World exports to China increased tenfold in real terms from 1985 to 2006, starting at $34 billion in the mid-1980s and reaching $384 billion by 2006. One of the most marked changes, especially in just over the last decade, is that developing countries have become a significant factor in China trade. We look at the origin of Chinese imports in three years: 1995, 2000, and 2006. While developing countries in 1995 comprised only 14.3 percent of the $83 billion of global exports to China, by 2006 they were supplying China with 50.3 percent of its $384 billion of imports. The opposite, of course, happened with the developed world. Whereas the developed world was once the chief exporter to China (85 percent in 1995), developed countries now supply just under half of all exports to China.

Developing countries have also become the largest commodities exporters to China. In 1995 developed countries supplied 68.6 percent of all commodities exports to China, but by 2006 that share stood at only 38.8 percent. Developing countries accounted for only 31.4 percent of commodities exports to China in 1995 and by 2006 supplied 61.2 percent of those exports, a 29.7 percentage point change (PPC) over the period. Looking at the regional composition of that trade, we find that the majority of that change has been captured by countries in the former Soviet sphere of influence (14.4 PPC), sub-Saharan Africa (5.9 PPC), Latin America and the Caribbean (5.6 PPC), and South Asia (4.9 PPC). However, in the most recent period, between 2000 and 2006, LAC captured the majority of gains. By 2006, just over 40 percent of all commodities exports to China were from East Asia and the Pacific, 22 percent from LAC.

Direct Effects

In terms of China's demand for LAC's exports, its unprecedented economic growth and entry into the World Trade Organization have had direct and indirect effects on LAC's export and growth performances. Direct effects result from bilateral LAC-China trade. In-direct effects result from China's overall demand for LAC's top products and the extent to which that demand drives up prices for those products. We address each in turn.

Figure 2.1 exhibits LAC exports to China from 1985 to 2006 in broader context. Since 2000, those exports have grown by 370 percent, dwarfing the overall LAC export growth of 62.5 percent during the period. This fact and figure have fueled the optimism described earlier in the literature review, but it is often not discussed in its full context. Despite this astronomical growth, in 2006 LAC exports to China were still a mere 3.8 percent of all LAC exports. In other words, even after all that

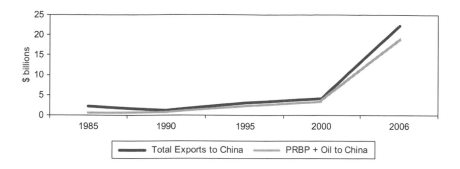

FIGURE 2.1 Latin American Exports to China (2005 dollars)
SOURCE: Authors calculations based on United Nations Statistics Division (2008).

growth, in 2006, 96.2 percent of all LAC exports did not go to China. Growth of exports to China did not even capture the lion's (or dragon's) share of LAC's export growth: growth in LAC exports to China was only 8 percent of all LAC export growth since the boom began in 2000.

On the other side of the story, China's imports from LAC were only 5.8 percent of total Chinese imports, the same level of LAC exports to China in the 1980s! Moreover, 74 percent of all China's imports from LAC were in primary commodities.

There is no doubt that China had a positive effect on LAC export growth during the boom, but how big was it? As we just showed, in terms of bilateral trade, the fanfare should be tempered. The large increase in LAC exports to China has barely held ground in terms of total Chinese import shares, and trade to China is a relatively small amount of total LAC exports. The significant growth in exports to China can almost exclusively be explained by China's emergence as a global trader. In addition, as we shall now see, only a handful of countries and sectors account for almost all of LAC's export surge to China. This may be the most salient yet overlooked characteristic of LAC-China trade.

The benefits of LAC-China trade are highly concentrated in a few countries and sectors. Table 2.1 reveals that in 2006 just ten sectors in six countries comprised 74 percent of all LAC exports to China and 91 percent of all LAC commodities exports to China. Indeed, the top five sectors—ores and concentrates of base metals (largely copper ores), soybeans, iron, crude petroleum, and copper alloys—were 60 percent

TABLE 2.1   Six Countries, Ten Sectors Dominate LAC Trade with China (percent)

Sector	Share of PRBP exports to China (2006)	Share of total LAC exports to China	Country (2006) (Country share of LAC exports to China in sector)
Crude petroleum	10.2%	8.3%	Argentina (43%), Brazil (41%)
Ores and concentrates of base metals	20.6%	16.7%	Chile (55%), Peru (32%)
Soybeans and other seeds	19.1%	15.6%	Brazil (63%), Argentina (37%)
Iron ore and concentrates	14.5%	11.8%	Brazil (90%)
Copper alloys	9.6%	7.8%	Chile (89%)
Soybean oil and other oils	3.9%	3.2%	Argentina (84%)
Nonferrous base metal waste and scrap	3.6%	2.9%	Mexico (45%), Colombia (29%)
Pulp and wastepaper	3.6%	2.9%	Brazil (53%), Chile (46%)
Feedstuff	3.2%	2.6%	Peru (66%), Chile (26%)
Meat	2.7%	2.2%	Brazil (88%)
Total	90.8%	73.9%	

SOURCE: Authors' calculations based on United Nations Statistics Division (2008).

of all exports to China and 75 percent of LAC commodities exports to China.

A mere handful of countries accounted for LAC exports to China in these ten commodities. The final column in table 2.1 exhibits the share of each exporting country of total LAC exports to China in a particular commodity. In other words, looking at the first row, Argentina and Brazil exported 43 and 41 percent respectively of all LAC crude petroleum exports to China (the majority of Venezuelan and Mexican oil exports are destined for the United States and do not reach China). Brazil alone exported 90 percent of all LAC exports of iron and 88 percent of all meat to China, Argentina exported 84 percent of all soybean oil.[1]

This table reveals that just six countries dominated the majority of LAC exports to China: Argentina, Brazil, Chile, Colombia, Mexico, and Peru. Four of the countries—Argentina, Brazil, Chile, and Peru—showed up as the most dominant exporters to China. Mexico and Colombia accounted for the majority of exports of nonferrous metal waste and scrap metal to China, but did not make a significant contribution to China exports in any other sector. Other research that has compared the export basket of various LAC countries with the import potential of China found that for countries and sectors other than those on this list, the potential for trading with China in the future is very low (Blázquez-Lidoy, Rodríguez, and Santiso 2006).

Finally, for the four major countries and sectors identified in table 2.1 we calculate, for the most relevant sectors, the share of exports that go to China (table 2.2). For some sectors China exports are a very large part of a country's total exports in a sector and a large percentage of total LAC exports in that sector.

TABLE 2.2 Share of China Exports in Selected Countries and Sectors, 2006

Country, Sector	Exports to China in Sector (USD 2005)	% Total Country Exports in Sector
Argentina		
Crude petroleum	875,806,061	37
Soybeans and other seeds	1,390,304,704	73.7
Soybean oil and other oils	645,112,304	18.2
Brazil		
Oil	818,654,645	12
Soybeans and other seeds	2,381,576,901	42.7
Iron	2,575,374,873	37.8
Pulp and paper	372,549,748	5.5
Meat	464,630,823	6.5
Chile		
Copper ores	2,205,461,023	16.2
Copper alloys	1,692,789,989	8.5
Pulp and paper	325,269,717	24.8
Feedstuff	169,337,323	31.4
Peru		
Copper ores	1,303,296,018	22.4
Feedstuff	423,127,024	36.3

SOURCE: Authors' calculations based on United Nations Statistics Division (2008).

To be clear, table 2.2 examines the percent of exports in a particular sector that go to China (whereas table 2.1 exhibits the China share of total LAC exports in a given sector and the country share of total LAC exports in a sector).

Table 2.2 shows that China trade has dominated exports in some of these sectors. What stands out most is that 73.7 percent of all soybeans exported from Argentina were destined for China and that 42.7 percent of all soybeans exported from Brazil went to China as well; 37.8 percent of all Brazil's iron exports went to China. Only in the case of Brazil's pulp and paper and meat sectors and Chile's copper alloy sector were China exports less than 10 percent of each country's total exports in those sectors.

It should come as no surprise, then, that these countries and sectors are the major recipients of foreign direct investment (FDI) from China (Ellis 2008). FDI from China grew significantly between 1990 and 2005, reaching $12.6 billion in 2005 (Devlin 2008). Table 2.3 exhibits 2006 (the same year as data in tables 2.1 and 2.2) investments in Argentina, Brazil, Chile, and Peru.

In spite of these trends, there has been some concern in the region that China is taking away FDI from LAC. However, according to econometric exercises by the World Bank, China is not displacing FDI from LAC. Indeed, OECD stocks of FDI in LAC were bigger than those in China, when scaling for GDP (Cravino, Lederman, and Olarreaga 2009). Such analyses make perfect sense. China is rapidly industrializing, and therefore one would expect investment in China to follow that growth. As China industrializes, it needs more primary commodities for inputs to the industrialization process and for a changing diet, which creates more demand for nations such as those in LAC with those commodities. Investors then pour investment into Chinese manufacturing and LAC commodities.

Indirect Effects

Indirectly, during the boom, increases in Chinese demand tightened supplies and raised global prices for many commodities, leading to a rise in exports. More directly of course, China's appetite for commodities has increased bilateral trade between LAC and China. This result in part drove up prices for LAC goods (International Monetary Fund 2008). But China is only one part of the commodities boom. High prices enjoyed

TABLE 2.3 Major 2006 Chinese Investments in LAC

(Argentina)

In February 2006, the periodical *Business News Americas* announced that Chinese steel trading company Sinosteel Corporation was considering an undisclosed but significant investment in the Argentine iron ore miner Hiparsa with the express purpose of increasing iron ore production to meet Chinese demand. Separately, in the transportation sector, the Chinese have discussed participation in improving the Cristo Redentor and Aguas Negras passes. The passes are key choke points on highways used to ship Argentine products over the Andes mountains for ultimate export via Chile's Pacific ports. In the winter, snows routinely close the passes, delaying the transit of Argentine products to destinations such as China.

(Brazil)

Chinese deals and acquisition activity have focused on Brazil's iron and steel and petroleum sectors. With respect to the former, the Chinese firm Baosteel and the Brazilian firm Companhia Vale do Rio Doce (CVRD) began talks in July 2004 to construct an iron ore production facility in Brazil. CVRD was subsequently rumored to be in joint venture talks with the Chinese firm Minmetals, although no concrete deals have emerged as of the time that this article went to press [see Source]. In February 2006, Metals and the Metallurgical Construction Group of China finalized a deal providing Gerdau S.A. $235 million to increase its steelmaking capacity in Brazil. With respect to petroleum, in November 2004 the Brazilian state firm Petrobras signed a $10 billion commitment to cooperate with the Chinese firm Sinopec in prospecting for oil, refining, and constructing pipelines in Brazil. Subsequently, in July 2005, Petrobras signed a long-term contract to sell 12 million barrels of oil per day to the PRC firm Sinochem for $600 million. In addition to these commitments, China has proposed $4.8 billion in investments to modernize the Brazilian railway system—facilitating Brazil's ability to get its iron ore, steel, and other products to market for export to destinations such as the PRC.

(Chile)

In February 2006, China Minmetals and China Development Bank finalized a deal providing the Chilean state copper company Codelco with up to $2 billion in financing through advance commodity purchases so that Codelco could increase its mining capacity for export to China. Codelco is the world's largest copper supplier, while the PRC is Chile's number one export customer. The deal also included an option to sell Minmetals a 25–49% interest in the new Gaby mineral field for an additional $900 million.

(Peru)

On February 27, 2006, the Peruvian congress approved a massive project in which the Chinese consortium Shandong Luneng would invest $2 billion to significantly upgrade the port facility at Tacna, and another $8 billion to build new highway and rail links connecting Tacna to the El Mutún mineral field in eastern Bolivia. Shandong Luneng is also one of the major bidders for the El Mutún concession, which has been repeatedly delayed by the Bolivian government. Securing both projects would thus give a major PRC firm an integrated supply network for extracting iron from the region. In addition to Tacna, another $300 million in smaller PRC investment projects are also contemplated for the Peruvian mining, petroleum, and fishing industries. In the hydrocarbon sector the Chinese position in Peru was also bolstered by the China National Offshore Development Corporation (CNODC) purchase of a 45% interest in PlusPetrol Norte, a subsidiary of the Argentine firm PlusPetrol. The acquisition has given China a presence in the Camisea gas fields—a project that has recently come on-line and is significantly boosting Peru's natural gas output, and rapidly making Peru a significant player in the region's natural gas supply.

SOURCE: Ellis (2006), http://www.airpower.maxwell.af.mil/apjinternational/apjs/2006/3tri06/elliseng.html, quoted verbatim.

by LAC exporters of commodities were also the result of supply limitations and speculation. Regardless of the driver, in the end, per capita growth for the big LAC exporters to China was not significantly different than per capita growth for LAC nations that did not have a significant amount of exports destined for China (World Bank 2009).

Table 2.4 shows the modest impacts China has had on the exports of LAC's top export commodities. The table lists LAC's top seventeen

TABLE 2.4   Latin America's Top Commodities Exports in Context

Sector	2000	2006	2000–06 Growth (%)	Chinese Import Growth/Total World Export Growth (%)
		(2005 USD)		
Crude oil	48,987,186,770	112,575,599,155	129.8	5.5
Base metals	7,211,709,637	26,183,980,627	263.1	19.7
Copper	7,628,915,967	25,749,477,183	237.5	10.8
Refined petroleum	16,620,782,467	18,806,398,334	13.1	5.2
Meat	3,535,083,967	11,070,973,817	213.2	–1.6
Iron ore and concentrates	3,811,562,912	9,425,950,165	147.3	54.8
Feedstuff	6,413,819,994	9,414,473,361	46.8	2.6
Fruit and nuts	6,609,994,529	9,214,179,325	39.4	0.1
Sugar and honey	3,293,727,533	8,358,410,784	153.8	1.8
Soybeans	4,155,155,048	8,209,199,475	97.6	57.8
Natural gas	1,422,921,528	8,053,331,973	466.0	1.8
Coffee and coffee substitutes	6,320,846,594	7,400,327,391	17.1	1.5
Vegetable oils, crude or refined	2,413,049,966	5,123,976,205	112.3	8.4
Aluminium	3,211,590,964	4,533,157,750	41.1	1.4
Fresh vegetables	3,322,155,825	4,531,071,548	36.4	4.2
Alcoholic beverages	2,757,791,184	4,188,139,047	51.9	2.5
Fish, fresh, chilled, or frozen	2,551,440,823	3,982,054,605	56.1	9.3
Pulp and wastepaper	3,325,463,834	3,915,651,191	17.7	118.9
Average	7,421,844,419	15,596,463,996	110	17

SOURCE: Authors' calculations based on United Nations Statistics Division (2008).

export commodities sorted by their total value (in dollars) in 2006. These top exports were just shy of half of all LAC's exports during the period and grew an average of 110 percent between 2000 and 2006. Far and away the largest export was crude oil, which alone accounted for more than 18 percent of all LAC exports.

The last column in table 2.4 exhibits the share of Chinese import growth as a percent of world export growth in a particular sector. It shows that China accounted for less than one-fifth of the growth in the seventeen sectors that LAC exports the most. Base metals, copper, iron ore, soy, meat, feedstuff and pulp and paper are all highlighted in bold because they are among the core LAC exports to China that are discussed above. Chinese demand for global exports in these products was quite high, with 54 percent of the increase in world iron ore exports going to China, 57.8 percent of all soy, and more than 118.9 percent of pulp and paper.[2]

In other words, indirectly through increased demand and the resulting price increases, China was indirectly responsible for much of Latin America's commodity export boom. World Bank economists have done econometric analyses that confirm this relationship. According to their calculations, soybean prices have the strongest and most statistically significant correlation with Chinese demand (Calderón 2009). Some sectors are well below the average. Chinese imports of crude petroleum, for example, account for 5.5 percent of the growth in exports between 2000 and 2006.

The analysis conducted in this part of the chapter has shown that China is having a significant impact on LAC, but not necessarily in all the ways portrayed by some. Many countries simply do not export the goods that China impacted directly through global demand and price increases or through bilateral trade. In addition, only ten sectors in six countries account for the majority of China-LAC trade during the boom. For those six countries and ten sectors that account for the majority of China-LAC trade during the boom, China indeed both propped up world prices and accounted for a significant part of the export increase in those countries.

Even in soybeans, however, China accounted for just over half of LAC exports. Other factors were also involved. LAC exports also surged because of low interest rates and higher demand in the United States. In the case of sectors such as soybeans, the shift in the United States to corn-based ethanol also shortened supply in that sector and therefore led to price rises as scarce corn was substituted by soybeans. Market power and pure speculation were also to blame, especially in the post-2005 period. Some go so far as to argue that speculation was the main contributor to the commodity price boom (Wray 2008).

Now that the boom has come to a halt, it worth analyzing whether it also posed a development challenge to Latin America. To this question we now turn.

Is the Future So Bright?

These findings raise a number of concerns regarding China's impact in Latin America that run counter to the more euphoric tone about the LAC-China relationship found in the popular press and some of the literature during the boom. There are three key questions of concern that need to be addressed by researchers and policymakers. For the small number of LAC countries that are benefiting from China trade:

1. Beyond the boom, how long can LAC depend on increasing Chinese demand for LAC commodities, and similarly, to what extent—in the long term—will prices for such commodities remain high?
2. To what extent will future China trade result in a "resource curse" problem for LAC, given that China trade is largely in commodities?
3. How well are LAC governments equipped to capture increased revenues from growing commodities exports, and are the revenues being used to stabilize and diversify the economy?

There are some grounds for optimism on all three levels. Estimates conducted before the outset of the financial crisis concluded that for the export sectors most important to China, Chinese demand would continue its rise for some time to come. Regarding Dutch disease, where primary commodity-dependent countries do not develop strongly because they are victims of a "resource curse," there is cause for concern, but more research is needed. During the period analyzed, there was a slight appreciation in the currencies of the four key countries relative to others in LAC. There is also some evidence that export surges to China are taking a heavy toll on the environment. On the question of revenue gains, because of past crises LAC has considerably more institutions that can capture gains from commodities booms, but, with a few exceptions, the purse strings are being held tight as LAC nations respond to the crisis. Nevertheless, LAC has a better opportunity than it has had in decades, even in the wake of the crisis. In the last chapter of this book, we argue that this opportunity needs to be seized.

The Future of Chinese Demand and High Commodities Prices

Before the financial crisis hit, economic growth in China was expected to continue its unprecedented expansion for at least another decade. Estimates of Chinese economic growth have been corrected downward in light of the economic crisis, but they still hover at 8 percent or more. High prices for commodities are another matter, however. Most forecasts estimate that the recent commodity boom was fairly unique and may last longer than those in the past—but not forever. Such projections, however, are pre-crisis, and prices have been pushing downward since 2008. If the crisis teaches us anything, however, it is that booms and busts are prevalent. Any future booms are indeed opportunities for those countries benefiting from them, but they will not be if nations do not act quickly.

Forecasting future Chinese growth has become a cottage industry, but most conservative forecasts put annual growth rates for China between 7.1 and 8.6 percent to 2020 (Jianwu, Li, and Polaski 2007). In 2006 Deutsche Bank Research put together estimates of future Chinese demand in key commodities from Africa and South America. Deutsche Bank projects increased demand for all of the important sectors analyzed in the previous section. Indeed, table 2.5 shows that in every sector except for soy, pre-crisis estimates of future growth exceed 10 percent per annum.

The Deutsche Bank Research team argues that soy demand will not be as significant as in other sectors:

> Soy imports have risen steadily as domestic production struggles to fulfill rising demand. Growth in soybean demand has been mainly driven by increased consumption of soybean oil and soybean meal

TABLE 2.5 Projections for China's Commodity Import Demand

| | Annual Demand | | Percent Change, 2006–2020 | |
| | 2006 | 2020 | | |
Commodity	(m tons)		Total	Annual
Oil	91	1,860	1,940	20
Iron	148	710	380	10
Soy	26	50	80	4
Copper	3	20	600	10
Meat	0.3	4	1,260	20
Pulp and Paper*	34	150	330	10

*m cubic meters
SOURCE: Deutsche Bank Research (2006).

(both outputs of the crushing process). Especially demand for soybean meal—which is used to feed livestock and is thus driven by demand for meat—was a major driver of Chinese soybean import growth. This makes future Chinese demand for soybeans difficult to predict. While human consumption of soybeans and soybean oil is likely to increase further, demand growth for soybean meal could decrease as livestock cultivation faces limits and imports of meats and other animal products gain ground. Therefore, overall demand growth for soybeans is likely to lag behind other commodities. (Deutsche Bank Research 2006, 5)

Although soy demand is predicted to grow the slowest, table 2.5 shows it is still predicted to almost double by 2020. Doubling is quite large but seems smaller given that other commodities such as meat and crude oil are expected to grow by a factor of three or more.

Chinese growth may continue for the foreseeable future (even during the heat of the crisis, China grew by over 6 percent in 2008 and 2009), but high prices for commodities in general may not (OECD and FAO 2009). The International Monetary Fund (IMF) reminds us that although the prices for commodities have been high, they remain below their historical levels, are highly volatile, and over the long term are predicted to continue their downward trend. Since 1957 commodity prices have fallen relative to consumer prices at a rate of about 1.6 percent annually.

However, volatility is more the norm than price decline—one standard deviation of annual price changes is close to 11 percent, compared to the 1.6 percent annual decline. The IMF attributes such falls to productivity gains in the agricultural and metals parts of the economy relative to others (International Monetary Fund 2006).

Figure 2.2 exhibits declining nonenergy prices (on the first vertical axis) with the downward trend line in jagged black. Terms of trade in Latin America are scaled to the second vertical axis and are also declining over the long term. This long-term deterioration in the terms of trade for commodities has been thoroughly documented for a longer period of time (see Ocampo and Parra 2003 for an analysis for the whole twentieth century) and has been a core concern for long-term development in Latin America since the formulation of the Prébisch-Singer hypothesis, which states that the terms of trade between primary products and manufactured goods tend to decline in the long run (Prébisch 1951).

However, it is quite clear that both prices and the terms of trade for Latin America increased from 2000 until before the crisis. The IMF does

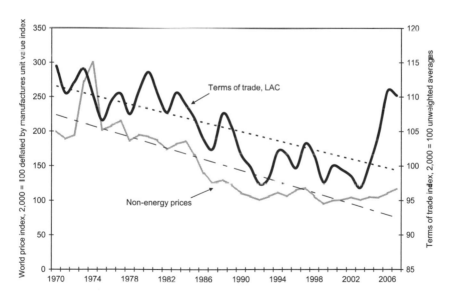

FIGURE 2.2 World Commodities Prices and LAC Terms of Trade, 1970 to 2007
SOURCE: International Monetary Fund (2008).

acknowledge that the recent boom was one of the longest and largest in recorded history. For the average country the boom lasted over four years and caused an improvement in the terms of trade by 9 percent, while past booms lasted on average two years and changed terms of trade by 3 percent (International Monetary Fund 2008). Before the crisis, some analysts forecasted price increases through 2015. The International Food Policy Research Institute predicted that soy and soy oils would see significant increases until that year (International Food Policy Research Institute 2008). However, the crisis changed the scenario. As figure 2.3 shows, between 2008 and 2009 prices for most commodities started to slide at significant levels.

A closer look at the specific sectors benefiting from China trade shows a slightly different pattern. The long-term trend for the agricultural commodities slopes downward, but the trend for nonrenewable natural resources was on the rise until the crisis (Figure 2.2). Indeed, the bump up since 2002 in figure 2.2 seems to be in large part a function of copper, iron, and pulp and paper prices, not agricultural ones.

The big question before the crisis was how long the increase in commodity prices and the resulting improvement of terms of trade would actually last, and whether these improvements will reverse the downward

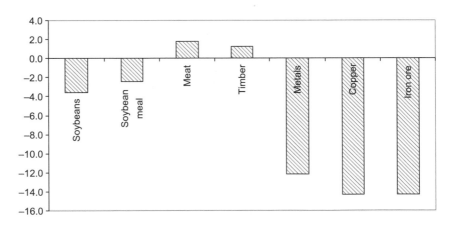

FIGURE 2.3 Estimated Price Decreases, 2008–2009 Percentage Variation
SOURCE: International Monetary Fund (2009).

trend observed since the beginning of the twentieth century (Ocampo and Parra 2003). In fact, while the small range of estimates available quibble over how long price increases will last, even before the crisis there was consensus that they would eventually decline and that the commodity boom would not put LAC on the verge of long-term economic growth with current-account surpluses (International Monetary Fund 2006; Ocampo 2007).

Nevertheless, through 2009 China continued to import key LAC commodities and invest in LAC as well. To take advantage of lower prices and to diversify its dollar holdings, China began purchasing significant amounts of LAC copper and iron in 2009. Chinese FDI and financing have also ticked upward, with China investing in Mexican steel and providing a $10 billion loan to Brazil's oil firm, Petrobras (Romero and Barrionuevo 2009; Bradsher 2009a).

LAC, China, and the Resource Curse

Tangential but important to this discussion is the extent to which China's small but important tug on the LAC export basket will inflict the region with Dutch disease. Nations overly dependent on commodities have been shown to deindustrialize because discoveries of such resources and their subsequent export raise the value of a nation's currency and make manufactured and agricultural goods as well as services less competitive, eventually increasing imports, decreasing exports, creating balance-of-payments problems, and leading to poor economic performance (Sachs and Warner 1995).

At this writing the prospects of LAC's being inflicted by Dutch disease are speculative at best. However, such speculation is a result of a stack of fairly plausible scenarios that are worth mentioning here, especially given the fact that once again LAC has gone through yet another commodities boom.

If future demand from China and the indirect effect that China demand may have on higher commodities prices in general rebounds, it is possible that some Latin American countries will have larger shares of primary and resource-based products in their export baskets. During 2002–2007 there was only slight (if any) evidence of a resource curse. If we were to observe Dutch disease, we would expect to see appreciating exchange rates and declining shares of manufacturing as a percent of GDP.

In the boom period, 2002–2007, there was a significant appreciation of the currency in most LAC countries except in the relatively more manufacturing-centered nation of Mexico. Figures for industrial structure reveal that at present there has been no significant change—except in the case of Chile. In Brazil and Peru, manufacturing as percent of GDP has remain unchanged since 1993, and in Argentina there has been an increase by almost five percentage points. In Chile, however, manufactures were 18.1 percent of GDP in 1995 and 15.7 percent of GDP in 2007. Of course, whether looking at exchange-rate changes or changes in industrial structure, these trends may be related to China in no way whatsoever. Such analyses are beyond the scope of this book but should be examined in detail for future research. The point here is that presently there are no noticeable changes that would make one cry "Resource curse," but theoretically the possibility remains.

The resource curse has traditionally examined exchange rates, export diversity, and growth—and not the environmental implications of resource-based growth. Barbier (2004) extends the resource-curse analysis for Latin America and shows that this problem has plagued Latin America in the past and that because of LAC's skewed distribution of wealth and poverty, it has also exacerbated environmental degradation and social inequity during commodity booms. Barbier shows how LAC has often experienced growth through "frontier land expansion" but that in the end such expansion did not generate rents substantial enough to be reinvested in other productive activities, nor does it generate enough linkages and productivity spillovers to achieve broad-based, sustainable growth. How and why does this happen? LAC attracts investors in commercial agriculture, mining, and timber extraction, and these investors tended to be among the more wealthy people in the country or across the globe. Such intensive extractive activity and actors in the "frontier," along with the accompanying pressure from population increases and water use, leads to excessive resource conversion.

According to Barbier, significant rents did not accrue over the long run—though there are undoubtedly booms—because the resources got depleted over time and because of government and market failures in the form of rent seeking, corruption, and open-access problems. The limited rents that did accrue were seldom redistributed for more dynamic economic activity (nor invested in natural capital or the poor) because these actors benefit from rent-seeking activities resulting from further frontier expansion. What is more, to Barbier, resource-based activities essentially became rural enclaves far away from centers that could form significant backward linkages or knowledge spillovers. The rents that did accrue went to wealthy individuals, who have increased incentive for "rent-seeking" behavior that is in turn supported by policy distortions that reinforce the existing pattern of allocating and distributing natural resources.

Figures 2.4 and 2.5 exhibit how this may have occurred recently in Brazil with respect to frontier soy expansion in Brazil. Remember from table 2.2 that 42.7 percent of all Brazilian soy exports (over 20 percent of total soy production) is destined for China. Figures 2.5 and 2.6 exhibit the expansion of soybean production into the environmentally sensitive Amazon region between 1990 and 2005. In 1990, 88 percent of

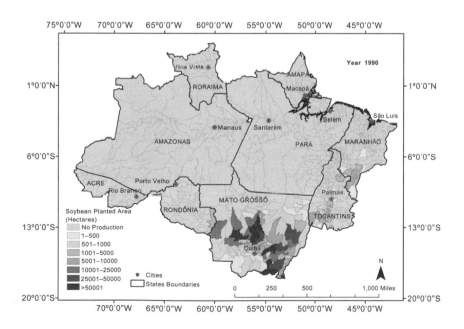

FIGURE 2.4 Soy Expansion in the Amazon, 1990
SOURCE: Vera-Diaz et al. (2008).

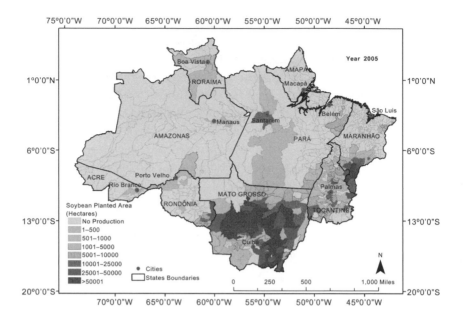

FIGURE 2.5 Soy Expansion in the Amazon, 2005
SOURCE: Vera-Diaz et al. (2008).

all soy production was located in the state of Mato Grosso. However, by 2005 that figure was only 40 percent, and soy production had expanded into Maranhao, Para, Acre, Roraima, and Rondonia.

Alongside the possibility of exchange rate appreciation and environmental degradation, Dutch disease could also cause a lack of competitiveness for noncommodity sectors. Here a great deal of work has been conducted comparing China and LAC and the extent to which China will outcompete LAC in world markets. In other words, is China penetrating (or does it have the potential to penetrate) world export markets at a faster rate than firms in LAC? We dedicate the rest of the volume to this question.

Revenue Sharing, Stabilization, and Diversification

How equipped are LAC nations to using booms as an opportunity to diversity their economies and buffer them from future busts? Related to the promise of high prices and future demand from China is the question regarding whether Latin American nations are equipped to capture the rents from such high prices and demand and to use them for responding to crises, for general savings, and for economic diversification (Rodrik 2005; Cypher 2007).

Recent studies have conducted fairly comprehensive examinations of these questions. The results are mixed. On the one hand, all of the major commodities exporting countries to China have seen increases in revenue and reserves due to high export prices and overall increases in the volume of trade. Moreover, many of the countries have created new funds and laws that govern the use of revenue derived from price increases in commodities exports (Ocampo 2007). However, with the exception of Chile these funds have not played a significant role in crisis recovery. Leading up to and after the crisis there is little indication that such funds will be used for economic diversification and poverty alleviation. Indeed, in the wake of the crisis the majority of these funds have been used to defend currencies and bail out banking systems.

The large price increases and increases in demand for primary-commodity and resource-based exports in the countries analyzed above have led to a significant increase in government revenue. Because of new tax schemes and funds, the majority of countries in LAC have increased fiscal revenues by 3 percent of GDP or more (Jiménez and Tromben 2006).

In Brazil, government revenues have actually become positive since 1999 and reached a maximum surplus of 4.6 percent of GDP in 2004. In Brazil's case, however, fiscal revenue increases have largely been a result of economic growth, a diversified tax base, and reductions in spending. In other words, the commodities boom contributed very little either positively or negatively to Brazil's fiscal position (Gottshalk and Prates 2006). In 2008, Argentina attempted to increase an already sizable export tax on agricultural exports, yet such an increase was met by widespread discontent and farmer riots and forced the government to partially back down.

In the case of Chile, however, the situation is different. Chile's government revenues have grown significantly, which has been chiefly due to higher copper revenues. Chile also had a fiscal surplus in 2004 of 2.2 percent of GDP. Between 1999 and 2004, copper explained 29.3 percent of total government revenue, but 59 percent for 2003 and 2004. The share of copper revenues in government revenue was 2.4 percent from 1999 to

2002, but leapt to between 12.6 and 17.6 percent in 2004. The state-owned copper company CODELCO (while only 37 percent of copper production) accounted for 75 percent of government revenues from copper in 2004 (Gottshalk and Prates 2006). Chile's copper funds have for several years been in part appropriated into the Copper Stabilization Fund, which was established in 1986 to smooth public spending from the variation in copper prices in the form of countercyclical macroeconomic policy.

In 2006, Chile's Fiscal Responsibility Law created two new sovereign funds: the Pension Reserve Fund (PRF) and the Economic and Social Stabilization Fund (ESSF). While the purpose of the PRF is to support the sustainability of Chile's old-age and disability pensions, the purpose of the ESSF is to enable Chile's government to conduct countercyclical macroeconomic policy. According to Chile's Ministry of Finance, the ESSF was created:

> To finance the fiscal deficits that may occur during periods of weak growth and/or low copper prices and can also be used to pay down pubic debt. In this way, it helps to reduce cyclical variations in fiscal spending, ensuring long-term financing for social programs. (Ministry of Finance [Chile] 2009)

The ESSF was initially capitalized with US$2.58 billion, most of which (US$2.56 billion) came from the Copper Stabilization Fund that the ESSF replaced.

To understand the process of capitalization of the ESSF, it is first important to understand Chilean fiscal policy. What enables Chile to save in times of bonanza is a rule establishing that annual fiscal spending will be calculated in accordance with "the central government's structural income, independently of fluctuations in revenues caused by cyclical swings in economic activity, the price of copper and other variables that determine effective fiscal income" (Ministry of Finance (Chile) 2009).

As a result, in years when Chile has a fiscal surplus, the Fiscal Responsibility Law establishes that after contributions to the PRF (which have to be between 0.2% and 0.5% of GDP) and the five-year (2006–10) capitalization of Chile's Central Bank (in an amount that is the difference between the capitalization of the PRF and the effective fiscal surplus, with an upper limit of 0.5% of GDP), all remaining fiscal surplus must be paid into the ESSF. However, repayments of public debt and advanced payments into the ESSF during the previous year can be subtracted from this contribution.

The combination of the rules in Chile's Fiscal Responsibility Law and the economic growth experienced in the years preceding the boom (as well as the returns on the investments made) resulted in the resources of the ESSF increasing almost eightfold. By December 31, 2008, the ESSF was worth more than US$ 20 billion. As a result, in 2008, Chile became a net creditor for the first time in its history. In terms of the performance of the ESSF, in 2008 the investments made by the ESSF showed a return of 7.63 percent. The annualized net return accumulated from March 2007, when the ESSF stated operating, has been of 9.47 percent.

These returns are not only important as a measure of a successful investment policy. They also matter because they provide an opportunity to increase Chile's fiscal spending in a sustainable manner: the annual interest generated by the investments of the PRF and the ESSF is considered structural fiscal income and can therefore be contemplated in the budget.

When the crisis finally hit in 2009, Chile began using the assets in the ESSF to put in place a fiscal stimulus of US$4 billion. The fiscal stimulus, announced in January 2009, contained different kinds of measures: $700 million for investments in infrastructure; $1 billion destined for investments in CODELCO, the state-owned copper company; additional incentives for the forestry sector; a series of tax cuts for businesses (with an emphasis on small and medium enterprises); a rebate of the income tax for fiscal year 2010; additional benefits for poorer Chileans; and a package of incentives to boost hiring ("Stimulating" 2009; Palma and Ojeda 2009).

At the time of this writing, it was too early to tell whether the fiscal stimulus had achieved the objectives it set out to accomplish. The jury is still out on the effect of this fiscal stimulus both on the level of activity as well as on the finances of the government. However, for the purposes of this book, what is worth highlighting is Chile's ability to protect itself—with the creation of the Economic and Social Stabilization Fund—from Dutch disease–driven currency appreciations in terms of boom as well as from volatility of economic activity levels resulting from volatility in commodity prices in times of crisis. In other words, through the ESSF Chile was able to conduct responsible and timely countercyclical macroeconomic policy.

Unfortunately, Chile's fiscal stimulus was almost exclusively aimed at preventing a sharp drop in economic activity and did not contain long-term measures to promote innovation and industrial development. To the contrary, a large share of Chile's fiscal stimulus was aimed at Chile's traditional resource-based exporting sectors: mining and forestry. Nonetheless, the mechanism established to save during booms could point to a path for securing a sustained flow of resources—from, for example, the returns generated from sovereign funds—for economic diversification in other countries in the region. This is probably the most important lesson for a new boom.

Peru has also experienced a fiscal surplus during the boom years. Here, however, the share of the copper sector in total government revenue has not changed as dramatically as in Chile. Revenues from gold and copper revenues combined (separate statistics for copper are unavailable) explained 4.5 percent of the growth of central government revenue between 1999 and 2004 but rose to just 6.7 percent for 2004. In Peru, two private firms (Southern Peru Copper Corporation and Antamina) account for 74 percent of copper production. Though a 30 percent tax on profits has been the main source of government revenues, extractive industries are exempt from royalty payments and can deduct for infrastructure investments (Gottshalk and Prates 2006).

Before the crisis it was hard to tell whether such increases in revenue were being used for poverty alleviation or economic diversification. In all the countries in LAC that have experienced increases in tax revenue and reserves, such increases have not been matched by a proportional increase in spending during bad times. It was a profound success that such funds were earmarked in a countercyclical nature—taking in funds when prices, exports, and growth are relatively strong and spending when things begin to slow down. In other cases, there is evidence of new spending for social programs, but they are seen as being inefficiently run and therefore have not shown up with concrete results (Clements, Faircloth, and Verhoeven 2007).

Moreover, many of the countries' new funds were being spent to pay down debt and get to surplus status (as mentioned earlier surpluses have only recently been reached). Although the majority of countries have stabilization funds, virtually all of them have stipulations where these funds are precommitted for macroeconomic stabilization (Jiménez and Tromben 2006). One study concluded that "as a result, the population at large and the poor in particular have not seen the benefits of the export boom, at least not through higher government expenditures as a proportion of GDP, on social and other programs" (Gottschalk and Prates 2006, 18). Cypher (2007) has argued that the lack of forward thinking regarding the utilization of new revenues could plague LAC for decades to come unless some portion of the funds is used to diversify economic structure. Cypher depicts the present as an enormous opportunity, but the result of short-sightedness, he warns, will be a "primarization" of LAC that could leave the region vulnerable to underdevelopment.

Conclusion

In this chapter we sought to provide a more critical analysis of China's impact on the recent Latin American commodity boom. In the recent boom, Latin American export growth, which was considerably faster than GDP growth, was being driven by a commodities boom. Indeed, 70 percent of the growth in LAC exports was due to growth in commodities exports, and commodities exports comprised 74 percent of all LAC exports. China had both indirect and direct effects on this trend. Directly, LAC exports to China have increased by 370 percent since 2000. This was the cause of much cheer but should be analyzed with more scrutiny. Indirectly, Chinese consumption of global commodities was making them scarcer and boosting global prices and leading somewhat to more LAC exports—also not as much as at first glance.

This chapter has shown that LAC exports to China have been relatively small and had not significantly grown as a percent of total LAC exports. On the other side of the Pacific, China's LAC share of total imports was small and relatively unchanged as well. LAC exports to China were only 3.8 percent of all LAC exports. In other words, 96.2 percent of all LAC exports did not go to China. LAC's exports to China comprised 5.8 percent of Chinese imports, the same level of LAC exports to China in the 1980s; 74 percent of all LAC exports to China were in primary commodities; growth in LAC exports to China was only 8 percent of all LAC export growth since the boom began in 2000; ten sectors in six countries accounted for 74 percent of all LAC exports to China and 91 percent of all LAC commodities exports to China; for the other countries in LAC, the potential to trade with China is very low.

Here Imansu does it mean manufactured exports to China only account for 3.8% of LAC exports b/c the previous A was telling about the vast increase in commodity exports?

For the handful of countries that were "winning" the export game with China, will Chinese demand and high prices continue, and will such longer-term trends boomerang back to LAC in the form of Dutch disease? By all pre-crisis accounts, the commodities boom and Chinese demand were predicted to last relatively long, even though by early 2009 estimates it was already clear that the boom had come to a halt. Pre-crisis estimates predicted that the commodities boom would be among the longest in history by lasting perhaps another ten years. China demand for the products that LAC supplies is predicted to last at least twenty more years. It remains to be seen how these predictions fare in light of the recent economic and financial crisis.

Regarding Dutch disease, more research is needed to examine the significance of the China trade effect on LAC exchange rates and industrial composition. We do know that exchange rates are appreciating, and the remaining chapters in this book show that the few nations in LAC with manufacturing competitiveness are losing some of that competitiveness vis-à-vis China. Moreover, at least in Brazil, there is evidence of a "frontier land expansion" in the environmentally sensitive Amazon, due in part to China's demand for soy.

Research indicates that LAC is more equipped than in the past to capture some of the rent from the recent and potential commodities booms and to use some of those funds for crisis recovery, poverty alleviation, environmental protection, and industrial development. Almost all the countries that benefited have some sort of institutional structure in place for such activity, though few are showing signs of putting them to proper use at present. Yet in the current crisis environment, it is very unlikely that such funds will go toward longer-term structural concerns such as industrial diversification.

3   Lost in Translation?

China and the Competitiveness of Latin American Manufacturing

The last chapter showed that China's expansion has brought some benefits to a handful of countries in the LAC region in terms of increased commodities exports. This chapter examines the extent to which China's expansion in manufacturing capabilities benefits or damages LAC manufactures in both world and home markets. Confirming and expanding upon previous research, we show that China's industrial competitiveness is improving much faster than that of LAC at home and abroad. What is more, based on estimates of the potential threat from China, the worst may be yet to come for LAC. Our major and alarming finding in this chapter is that 94 percent of all LAC's manufacturing exports were "under threat" from their Chinese counterparts, representing 40 percent of all LAC exports.

This chapter is divided into four additional parts. The first part charts the growth of Chinese manufacturing with respect to world manufactures exports in order to set the proper context for our analysis of the relative competitiveness of each country. The second part outlines the two complementary methodological approaches used to analyze the relative competitiveness among nations and the specific literature on China. Part three gives an analysis of the relative competitiveness of China's and LAC's export manufacturing in world markets. Part four analyzes the impact of China on regional and home LAC markets.

The Growth of China and LAC Manufacturing Exports

Over the past twenty-five years there has been significant growth in the world economy, and that growth has been propelled alongside a surge in global manufacturing exports. The experiences of China and LAC did not deviate from that trend. Indeed they both manifest it. Yet, China's growth has been nothing short of extraordinary.

On the right-hand scale of figure 3.1 is exhibited the steep increase in world manufacturing exports from 1985 to 2006. The left-hand scale juxtaposes the experiences of China and LAC.

While the size of the global manufacturing export market in 1985 was approximately $952 billion, in 2006 the market grew to more than $7 trillion—a 674 percent increase. Within that burgeoning market, both Chinese and Latin American manufacturing exports also grew significantly, albeit in a completely different order of magnitude. Percentage-wise, Chinese manufacturing exports grew even faster than world manufactures exports, at 23,000 percent between 1985 and 2006. LAC exports also bucked the global trend by increasing by 1,168 percent. Part of this difference, of course, is explained by the fact that in 1985, Latin American manufacturing exports were significantly higher than Chinese exports,

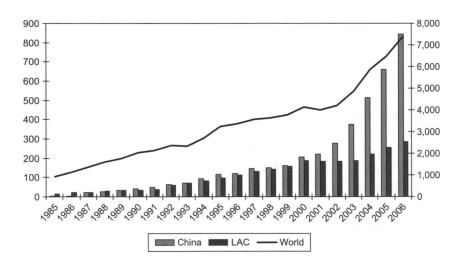

FIGURE 3.1 Manufacturing Exports (billions of current dollars)
SOURCE: Authors' calculations based on United Nations Statistics Division (2009).

with Latin America exporting more than $22 billion and China exporting only around $3.5 billion. However, that is only part of the picture.

Between 2000 and 2006, among all developing countries it was China that captured the greatest share of world growth in manufacturing during the period. Using the United Nations Statistics Division's "Commodity Trade Statistics Database" (COMTRADE), we calculated the regional and national share of total manufacturing export growth from 2000 to 2006. In other words, what was the share of specific countries and regions of total manufacturing export growth in the world economy during this period?

Interestingly, of the more than $6 trillion growth in manufacturing exports during the period, the Eurpean Union (EU) 15 captured the greatest share of the growth with 33 percent (of which 14.02 percentage points reflected growth captured by Germany). China accounted for 19.66 percent of the growth between 2000 and 2006. Indeed, China's growth was the largest gained by a single country and represented more than the growth captured by all the other countries in East Asia and the Pacific (including Japan) combined, which totaled 15.01 percent. The United States captured 4.76 percent; Latin America, as a whole, 3.02 percent, of which half was taken by Mexico (1.5 percent); and Brazil's share of the growth in manufacturing exports was shy of 1 percent.

China's unprecedented manufacturing expansion put it among world leaders in terms of export-led industrialization. Indeed, China leapfrogged like no other developing country in history. An interesting and telling index is the share of total exports that are manufacturing exports. In 1985, the world average for this index was 60 percent, with China at a mere 10 percent. By 2006 China's share had become the largest in the world, just short of 90 percent, with the world average lagging China at 63 percent. Mexico was the only nation in LAC at a level similar to China's, and has itself had a fairly spectacular move from 40 to 72 percent itself during the same period. Interestingly, both China and Mexico now enjoy similar shares of manufacturing in total exports to export powerhouse Germany. However, as we will see in Chapter 6, the nature of these manufactures is very different in China and Mexico, in that China's level of value-added and technological sophistication is increasing rapidly, while Mexico's is stagnating at relatively low levels. In Germany, of course, manufactures are of a very high value-added nature.

Estimating the Competitiveness of LAC Exports with China:
Previous Work

The question of how China's growth has impacted Latin American export competiveness is the subject of a burgeoning literature. Most earlier studies compared the export profiles of China and LAC to estimate the extent to which LAC *might* be threatened by China. However, this approach has been shown to have significant limitations, mainly because we currently have ample data to examine the actual levels of export penetration and competition between China and LAC.

Potential Impact: Comparisons of Export Structures

Most of the studies in the early part of the decade compared the export structures of China and the different countries in LAC. With the exception of Mexico and some Central American countries, the majority of these studies reached a rather optimistic view about the relative competitiveness of China and LAC in manufacturing. The nations of South America, it was held, exported a significantly different basket of goods to the world than China's. Therefore the exports of China and LAC could be seen as complementary rather than rival. However, more-recent studies that use this approach have come to different conclusions.

The comparison of export structures entails examining "the statistical correlation between the export structures of China and LAC (higher correlation indicates greater potential for competition and rising correlations over time suggest that the potential is growing)" (Lall and Weiss 2005, 169). Lall and Weiss compare the export structures of countries in LAC with that of China. They find that the only two countries whose export structure significantly correlates with China's are Mexico and Costa Rica (correlations are, respectively, 0.470 and 0.274). All other countries' correlations are 0.068 or less (Lall and Weiss 2005, 187).

Again, comparisons of export structure are based on the assumption that similar export structures will suggest the highest potential for competition. An earlier OECD study depicts the earlier consensus on this issue:

> In general terms, the results suggest that there is no trade competition between China and Latin America. . . . [Moreover] this trade competition is even decreasing rather than increasing over the recent period of

time. Not surprisingly, countries that export mainly commodities face lower competition. . . . Paraguay, Venezuela, Bolivia, and Panama are those that exhibit the lowest figures among 34 selected economies, i.e. those are the countries that suffer less from Chinese trade competition. Brazil could be considered as an intermediate case between Mexico and Venezuela. (Blázquez-Lidoy, Rodríguez, and Santiso 2006)

However, a more recent IDB study was the first to predict that the export structures of China and LAC may run into each other at some point. The IDB found that over time the two areas' export profiles were beginning to converge and overlap, and therefore fierce competition could ensue in the future: "As China and Latin America—and Mexico in particular— have converged toward increasingly similar export baskets, especially in manufacturing industries, direct competition has intensified" (Devlin, Estevadeordal, and Rodriguez-Clare 2006).

Very recent work compiled by the World Bank suggests that the IDB's predictions have come true, at least for some countries. Gordon Hanson and coauthor Raymond Robertson (2009) find that in Argentina, Brazil, Chile, and Mexico (LAC's main manufactures exporters), export capabilities were strong where China's were also strong. This suggests that the majority of LAC manufactures exports could potentially be under threat from China in both world and home markets. In summary, as the decade after China's accession to the WTO went on, and empirical research followed, China's potential threat seemed to be becoming a real one.

Actual Impacts

However, the methodology of comparing export structure has recently come under criticism in the peer-reviewed literature. Rhys Jenkins, for example, published a comprehensive analysis of such methodologies in the journal *World Economy* (2008). According to Jenkins, first, most analyses that compare export structures do not reflect the profound changes in China's exports after China's accession to the WTO in 2001, nor the entrance into force of the WTO's Agreement on Textiles and Clothing in 2005. Secondly, indexes that look at export structure normally only do so at one point in time and therefore overlook changes in the competitive threat of a nation over time. In other words, comparison of export structures look statically at what is a dynamic phenomenon. Third, export structure indices are weighted measures of the significance of the fit between two countries' export baskets.

Alternative measures have been deployed to look at actual changes in the competitiveness of China and LAC over time. Beyond merely comparing export structures, some authors have attempted to actually measure the observed impact of China's global export growth on Latin American manufacturing.

Lall and Weiss's approach is the one we use throughout this chapter and the next (for a detailed description, see technical appendix). These authors look at the evolution of China and LAC export shares in both the world and U.S. markets and look for evidence of increased Chinese competition in products that show increased penetration of Chinese exports in coincidence of decreased penetration of LAC exports. As we discuss in detail in the technical appendix to this volume, Lass and Weiss define a category (product sector) in which China's market share is rising (for either the world market or the U.S. market) and LAC's decreasing as a category in which LAC is experiencing a "direct threat" from China. Similarly, they define a category in which both China's and LAC's shares are increasing. but China's share is increasing faster as a category in which LAC is experiencing a "partial threat" from China.

Using this analytical framework, the authors argue that "for the world market for all the LAC 18 countries [in their study], the average weighted share of 'threatened exports'—under direct plus partial threat is surprisingly stable at 45.1% in 1990 and 39.4% in 2002." The authors also find the intensity of the Chinese threat, that is, the share of threatened exports that are "directly threatened," to decrease significantly over time and that, in 2002, only 11 percent of LAC exports are experiencing a "direct threat" (Lall and Weiss 2005. 178).

Using a very similar methodology,[1] Mesquita Moreira finds that "LAC losses to China in the world markets in 1990–2004 were on the whole relatively small, reaching 1.7% of the region's total manufacturing exports in 2004 (US$5.5 billion). As expected, given the differences in factor endowments, the highest losses were in low-tech, labor-intensive goods, which responded for nearly 30% of the total losses" (Mesquita Moreira 2007, 366). However, argues Mesquita Moreira, "the losses seen in the other categories reinforce the earlier argument that LAC should be prepared to face competition from China on the whole factor-intensity spectrum, from high-tech to natural resource-based manufactured goods" (2007)Moreover, losses have been mounting in the last years of the period. In a previous version of the same paper, which covered 1990–2002, Mesquita Moreira had found that the equivalent of 0.7 percent of the region's exports was being lost to China (Mesquita Moreira 2004). Adding two years to the analysis increased the figure to 1.7 percent.

Studies that use similar methodologies but with more recent data that reflect the post-WTO period come up with different findings than the earlier Lall and Weiss and Mesquita Moreira analyses. Jenkins (2009) deploys a "constant market share" method whereby countries gain from those nations where exports are growing more slowly, and lose to nations whose exports are growing faster. Analyzing the impact of China on LAC exports to the United States, Jenkins finds that contrary to export structure analyses, only Nicaragua and Peru have not lost exports in the U.S. to Chinese competition.

It must be underscored, however, that although these methods do a better job at taking a more dynamic view of relative competitiveness, they do not infer concrete evidence of causality between China's rise and LAC's corresponding decline. One study that does take a more dynamic approach and contains statistical analyses to determine the causality between China's export expansion and Mexico's decline was conducted by World Bank economist Caroline Freund. Freund and coauthor Caglar Ozden (2009) estimate with econometric techniques whether exports from China are displacing LAC's exports. The authors find that China's rise has a statistically significant and negative impact on Mexico's penetration of the U.S. market. Using data from 1985 to 2004, they also find that:

> (a) China's export growth has had only small effects on overall LAC exports, (b) China's export growth is primarily affecting Mexican export growth in industrial goods in Western Hemisphere markets, and (c) China's export growth is negatively affecting LAC exports of relatively high-wage goods. (Freund and Ozden 2009, 203)

In sum, despite earlier studies to the contrary, regardless of the methodology used, there is a growing concern of the extent to which China is outcompeting LAC in both U.S. and world markets, particularly in goods with a higher value added.

Competition in World Markets

In just over a quarter century, China went from insignificance to becoming the most competitive exporter of manufactures in the world. At the same time, most LAC nations remained marginal players, and those that gained some ground have struggled to maintain it. Only Mexico seems to be (somewhat) holding on.

Table 3.1 ranks the most competitive manufactures nations as measured by their share of total world manufactures exports every five years from 1980 to 2006. In terms of relative competitiveness, a quick look at the evolution of China's competitive position in comparative perspective highlights how dramatic China's gains in manufacturing competitiveness have been. Chinese growth has driven China to the second position in terms of manufacturing exports (table 3.1 also shows the evolution of manufacturing exports for the United States and Germany, the other major players in the manufacturing export market). If Hong Kong is counted (and China certainly counts it!), China has leapfrogged to become the most competitive manufacturer in the world.

Since 1980, China has steadily captured an ever increasing share of world manufacturing exports. While in 1985 China's manufacturing exports represented only 0.2 percent of world manufacturing exports, by 2006 China had become second only to Germany as an exporter of manufactures, with 11.5 percent of world manufacturing exports. Argentina and Brazil have somewhat maintained a small share of world manufacturing exports (around 1% for Brazil, 0.2% for Argentina) but have fallen down the export ladder as other countries have gained market share. Mexico, on the other hand, succeeded in increasing its share and climbing up the export ladder (going from 0.5% of world manufacturing exports in 1990 to 3.3% in 2000). Since 2000, however, Mexico's share and position as a manufacturing exporter have begun to erode again (reaching 2.5% of world manufacturing exports in 2006.)

Threat Analysis

How have Latin American countries competed with China in various manufacturing sectors since 2000? Not that well. We look at the competition between countries in LAC and China by contrasting the

TABLE 3.1 China: Taking Away the (Manufacturing) Ladder? (percent of world manufacturing exports)

1980		1985		1990		1995		2000		2006	
Fmr Fed. Rep. of Germany	17.0	Japan	17.2	Fmr Fed. Rep. of Germany	15.6	USA	12.8	USA	14.5	Germany	11.8
USA	15.4	Fmr Fed. Rep. of Germany	14.8	USA	13.0	Japan	12.4	Japan	10.4	**China**	**11.5**
Japan	13.8	USA	14.2	Japan	12.8	Germany	12.2	Germany	10.2	USA	10.2
France	8.4	France	6.6	France	6.9	France	6.1	France	5.3	Japan	7.5
United Kingdom	8.0	Italy	6.4	Italy	6.6	Italy	5.8	**China**	**5.0**	France	4.7
Italy	7.0	United Kingdom	6.1	United Kingdom	6.2	United Kingdom	5.2	Italy	4.7	Italy	4.4
Belgium-Luxembourg	4.2	Canada	4.5	Belgium-Luxembourg	3.6	China, Hong Kong SAR	4.8	United Kingdom	4.6	United Kingdom	4.1
Netherlands	3.6	Belgium-Luxembourg	3.2	China, Hong Kong SAR	3.5	**China**	**3.6**	China, Hong Kong SAR	4.5	China, Hong Kong SAR	4.0
Canada	2.8	Netherlands	3.0	Netherlands	3.2	Rep. of Korea	3.4	Canada	3.7	Rep. of Korea	3.7
Switzerland	2.5	Rep. of Korea	2.8	Canada	3.0	Belgium-Luxembourg	3.2	Rep. of Korea	3.6	Belgium	3.2
Sweden	2.4	China, Hong Kong SAR (Special Administrative Region)	2.8	Rep. of Korea	2.8	Canada	3.1	Mexico	3.3	Netherlands	2.9

(Continued)

TABLE 3.1 (*Continued*)

1980		1985		1990		1995		2000		2006	
China, Hong Kong SAR	2.0	Switzerland	2.2	Switzerland	2.3	Netherlands	3.0	Belgium	2.8	Singapore	2.7
Rep. of Korea	1.8	Sweden	2.1	China	2.0	Singapore	2.9	Singapore	2.7	Canada	2.5
Austria	1.5	Spain	1.5	Sweden	1.9	Switzerland	2.0	Netherlands	2.7	Mexico	2.5
Spain	1.5	Austria	1.3	Spain	1.8	Spain	1.9	Spain	1.9	Spain	1.9
Poland	1.2	Singapore	1.1	Singapore	1.7	Mexico	1.8	Malaysia	1.8	Switzerland	1.6
Denmark	1.0	Brazil	1.0	Austria	1.6	Malaysia	1.0	Switzerland	1.5	Malaysia	1.5
Singapore	0.9	Denmark	0.9	Denmark	0.9	Sweden	1.6	Sweden	1.4	Sweden	1.4
Finland	0.7	Finland	0.7	Malaysia	0.7	Austria	1.3	Thailand	1.2	Austria	1.3
Norway	0.6	Czechoslovakia	0.7	Brazil	0.7	Thailand	1.2	Ireland	1.1	Thailand	1.2
Ireland	0.4	Poland	0.6	Finland	0.7	Denmark	0.8	Austria	1.0	Czech Rep.	1.0
India	0.4	Ireland	0.6	Ireland	0.7	Ireland	0.8	Philippines	0.8	Poland	1.0
Australia	0.4	Norway	0.5	Thailand	0.6	Finland	0.7	Denmark	0.7	Turkey	0.9
Portugal	0.3	Turkey	0.5	Portugal	0.6	Brazil	0.6	Indonesia	0.7	Ireland	0.9
So. African Customs Union	0.3	Malaysia	0.4	Czechoslovakia	0.5	Portugal	0.5	Finland	0.7	India	0.8
Malaysia	0.3	Portugal	0.4	Mexico	0.5	Indonesia	0.5	Brazil	0.7	Brazil	0.8
Greece	0.2	India	0.4	Fmr Yugoslavia	0.5	India	0.5	India	0.6	Hungary	0.8
Argentina	0.2	China	0.4	India	0.4	Czech Rep.	0.5	Hungary	0.6	Denmark	0.7
Thailand	0.2	Israel	0.3	Norway	0.4	Turkey	0.5	Czech Rep.	0.6	Finland	0.7

Philippines	0.1	Australia	0.3	Turkey	0.4	Poland	0.4	Poland	0.5	Russian Federation	0.6
New Zealand	0.1	Thailand	0.2	Poland	0.3	Australia	0.4	Turkey	0.5	Philippines	0.5
Hungary	0.1	Greece	0.2	Australia	0.3	Israel	0.3	Russian Federation	0.5	Indonesia	0.5
Saudi Arabia	0.1	Pakistan	0.2	Israel	0.3	Norway	0.3	Israel	0.4	Slovakia	0.4
Tunisia	0.1	Argentina	0.2	Indonesia	0.3	So. African Customs Union	0.3	Portugal	0.4	Portugal	0.4
China, Macao SAR	0.1	Venezuela	0.1	Pakistan	0.2	Hungary	0.2	Australia	0.3	Ukraine	0.3
Colombia	0.1	Philippines	0.1	Romania	0.2	Philippines	0.2	South Africa	0.3	Romania	0.3
Bangladesh	0.1	Saudi Arabia	0.1	Greece	0.2	Pakistan	0.2	Norway	0.2	South Africa	0.3
Peru	0.1	Indonesia	0.1	Argentina	0.1	Slovenia	0.2	Slovakia	0.2	Israel	0.3
Indonesia	0.0	New Zealand	0.1	Philippines	0.1	Argentina	0.2	Ukraine	0.2	United Arab Emirates	0.3
Morocco	0.0	China, Macao SAR	0.0	Saudi Arabia	0.1	Slovakia	0.2	Pakistan	0.2	Australia	0.3
Cyprus	0.0	United Arab Emirates	0.0	United Arab Emirates	0.1	Romania	0.2	Argentina	0.2	Viet Nam	0.3
New Caledonia	0.0	Hungary	0.0	Tunisia	0.1	Greece	0.1	Romania	0.2	Norway	0.2
Kenya	0.0	Bangladesh	0.0	Morocco	0.1	Saudi Arabia	0.1	Slovenia	0.1	Saudi Arabia	0.2
Sri Lanka	0.0	Tunisia	0.0	New Zealand	0.1	Tunisia	0.1	United Arab Emirates	0.1	Slovenia	0.2
Syria	0.0	Morocco	0.0	China, Macao SAR	0.1	Croatia	0.1	Vietnam	0.1	Pakistan	0.2
Mauritius	0.0	Colombia	0.0	Venezuela	0.1	New Zealand	0.1	Luxembourg	0.1	Argentina	0.2

SOURCE: Authors' calculations based on United Nations Statistics Division (2009).

evolution of their market shares in a given period of time. We call the difference in market shares between the two years that limit the period "dynamic revealed competitive position" or DRCP (see appendix for full discussion).

For manufacturing as a whole, between 2000 and 2006 LAC's DRCP was –0.66 (its share in world manufacturing exports went from 4.53 to 3.87), while China's was 6.44 (it went from 5.03 to 11.47).

Table 3.2 exhibits our calculations, by country, on the percentage of manufacturing exports (to the world) that are under threat by China (see appendix for this chapter regarding the method for this calculation).

TABLE 3.2 Exports to the World, Percentage Threatened

	Direct	*Partial*	*Total*
Argentina			
As % of manufacturing exports in 2006	37	59	96
As % of all exports in 2006	10	16	27
Brazil			
As % of manufacturing exports in 2006	20	70	91
As % of all exports in 2006	9	30	39
Chile			
As % of manufacturing exports in 2006	29	53	82
As % of all exports in 2006	2	4	5
Colombia			
As % of manufacturing exports in 2006	15	66	81
As % of all exports in 2006	5	20	25
Costa Rica			
As % of manufacturing exports in 2006	36	60	96
As % of all exports in 2006	22	36	58
Mexico			
As % of manufacturing exports in 2006	70	28	99
As % of all exports in 2006	52	21	72
LAC			
As % of manufacturing exports in 2006	62	31	94
As % of all exports in 2006	27	14	40

SOURCE: Authors' calculations based on United Nations Statistics Division (2009).

walk me through how they come up with these figures?

For LAC as a whole we find that 62 percent of manufacturing exports fall under Lall's definition of a direct threat, and over 31 percent as a partial. Those manufacturing exports under threat represent *94 percent of all LAC's manufacturing exports and 40 percent of all LAC exports in 2006*, and add up to more than $260 billion.

For the largest manufacturers in the region, the threat level in world markets is significantly higher than the threat level in LAC markets, which we will look at in detail in the next section. Consistent with the literature on the subject, the situation for Mexico is the most grave. Ninety-nine percent of Mexico's manufacturing exports are under threat from China, representing 72 percent of Mexico's entire exports. Ninety-six percent of Costa Rica's exports are under threat, comprising 58 percent of all of Costa Rica's exports. Brazil and Argentina also see over 90 percent of their manufactures exports under threat, but those exports, as a share of total exports, are less than the LAC average, with 39 and 27 percent respectively.

In what sectors are these trends manifest and most acute? We looked in-depth at the top twenty Latin American manufacturing exports to find out. Several aspects are noteworthy about these top twenty categories. First, they represent 62.5 percent of all Latin American manufacturing exports. Moreover, in all but two of these twenty exports (pig and sponge iron, spiegeleisen, and ferro-alloys; polymerization and copolymerization products), Latin America is under threat from China. Of the top twenty Latin American manufacturing exports, the eighteen under threat from China also represent more than 60 percent of all Latin American exports under threat. Among these sectors are passenger cars, telecommunications equipment, auto parts, electronics, base metals, and more. Finally, it is worth noting that for the top twenty Latin American manufacturing exports, there is a heavy concentration in terms of suppliers. For most of these sectors, Mexico and Brazil are practically the only relevant players.

Competition in Regional LAC and Home Markets

Relatively little attention has been given to the extent to which China is threatening the competitiveness of LAC exports in Latin America itself, and even less regarding whether China is displacing LAC manufacturing firms in home markets. Initial analyses, including our own, suggest that the situation is not much better for LAC in this regard either.

The relative lack of attention to these matters is a problematic oversight, though admittedly it is due at least in part to data constraints. Latin America is an important anchor market for LAC manufacturing exports. What is more, like the world market, the LAC market has been growing as well. Between 1990 and 2006 LAC manufacturing import markets grew almost fivefold (497 percent, to be exact). More recently and specifically, between 2000 and 2006 the Latin American manufacturing import market grew 73 percent, while manufacturing imports from China grew 420 percent, capturing 21.5 percent of the total growth in Latin American manufacturing imports.

Indeed, the importance of looking at the impact of China's global export growth on Latin American manufacturing in Latin American markets stems from the fact that for Latin American exporters, regional markets absorb the largest share of their exports. This is particularly true in the case of manufacturing exports. As table 3.3 shows, for Argentina, Brazil, Chile, and Colombia, regional markets capture a significant share of their manufacturing exports (in all cases around half).

Moreover, in the cases of Argentina, Brazil, and Colombia, this reliance on the Latin American market for manufacturing exports has become more accentuated with time. While Argentina sent 31 percent of its manufacturing exports to Latin America in 1985, in 2006 this figure had reached 69 percent. For Brazil, while in 1985 only 16 percent of Brazil's manufacturing exports were destined for other parts of the LAC region, by 2006 this figure was 42 percent.

The reality for Costa Rica and Mexico is different. Costa Rica's dependency on the region has decreased to below the LAC average, and Mexico has never had any significant manufacturing exports flow to LAC. Argentina, Brazil, and Colombia are the cases where the reliance in the region is more pronounced and significantly above the regional average. While LAC's aggregate dependency on LAC markets for manufacturing has been significant (around 20% for the whole period), it never reached the levels of dependency observed in Argentina, Brazil, Chile, and Colombia.

How has, then, China's global export growth impacted Latin American manufacturing exports in Latin American markets? As we mentioned

TABLE 3.3 Exports to Latin America, Share of Total (percent)

	1985	1990	1995	2000	2006
Argentina					
Manufacturing	31%	39%	60%	64%	69%
Total	19%	26%	47%	48%	42%
Brazil					
Manufacturing	16%	18%	36%	37%	42%
Total	10%	11%	23%	25%	26%
Chile					
Manufacturing	63%	45%	67%	64%	52%
Total	15%	13%	19%	22%	17%
Colombia					
Manufacturing	45%	44%	62%	61%	59%
Total	12%	16%	28%	29%	31%
Costa Rica					
Manufacturing	58%	46%	62%	19%	19%
Total	17%	17%	21%	19%	18%
Mexico					
Manufacturing	6%	9%	5%	3%	5%
Total	6%	6%	5%	3%	5%
LAC					
Manufacturing	20%	21%	21%	14%	20%
Total	12%	14%	19%	16%	17%

*Data for 1985 was unavailable; 1985 calculation was performed with 1986 data.
SOURCE: Authors' calculation based on United Nations Statistics Division (2009).

earlier, there are very few analyses on this subject. One exception is new work by Eva Paus. Using a methodology that resembles the comparison of export structures discussed above, Paus estimates the degree to which China's exports might compete with Latin American imports and domestic production in the future. Paus constructs a "domestic competition index" (DCI), which measures the degree of correspondence between China's export structure and a Latin American country's import structure. Looking at this index, Paus concludes:

> What gives rise for concern is not the size of the DCI per se, but the fact that the DCI increased considerably in just four years. It suggests the

What is an export structure?

potential for domestic market competition from China may be rising substantially further in the future. (Paus 2009)

Conducting our threat analysis, we find that Chinese manufacturing exports are significantly threatening LAC manufacturing exports in LAC markets. As shown in table 3.4, the threat is particularly acute in the cases of Costa Rica and Mexico, albeit less important, given the relative minor importance of LAC's market for these two exporters (though, as we will see, these countries are getting clobbered in the U.S. market, which is of utmost importance for each). However, for Argentina, Brazil, Chile, and Colombia, the impact is significant. Between 2000 and 2006, 68 percent of what countries in Latin America imported in manufactures from Argentina was under threat from China (40% was "direct threat," 28%

TABLE 3.4 Exports to Latin America, Percentage Threatened

	Direct	Partial	Total
Argentina			
As % of manufacturing imports in 2006	40	28	68
As % of all imports in 2006	17	12	29
Brazil			
As % of manufacturing imports in 2006	9	36	45
As % of all imports in 2006	7	26	32
Chile			
As % of manufacturing imports in 2006	28	64	91
As % of all imports in 2006	5	13	18
Colombia			
As % of manufacturing imports in 2006	21	47	67
As % of all imports in 2006	12	27	39
Costa Rica			
As % of manufacturing imports in 2006	27	69	95
As % of all imports in 2006	20	51	70
Mexico			
As % of manufacturing imports in 2006	32	46	78
As % of all imports in 2006	26	38	65

SOURCE: Authors' calculations based on United Nations Statistics Division (2009).

"partial"). Moreover, threatened manufacturing imports from Argentina represented 29 percent of LAC's total imports from Argentina (that is, not only in manufacturing) in 2006. For Brazil—the other manufacturing powerhouse with a significant regional export bias—the figures are not that high, but albeit significant: 45 percent of what countries in Latin America imported in manufactures from Brazil was under threat from China, representing 32 percent of all LAC's imports from Brazil in 2006.

We also examine in more detail the sectoral composition of Latin American manufacturing imports from China. We conduct a threat analysis for the top twenty Latin American manufacturing imports from China, which account for more than 60 percent (61.8%, to be precise) of all Latin American manufacturing imports from China. Several elements are noteworthy. Latin American manufacturing imports from China grew much more between 2000 and 2006 than manufacturing imports from the rest of the world. In fact, while the rate of growth on average for the top twenty Chinese imports was 570 percent for China, it was only 89 percent for the rest of the world for those same twenty products.

Even less work has focused specifically on the impact of Chinese export expansion on domestic production. This is largely due to the difficulty in merging global trade data with domestic production data. A recent work coordinated by Jenkins (Jenkins 2009; López and Ramos 2007; Jenkins 2010) summarizes analyses that look at domestic markets in Argentina and Brazil. For Argentina, Jenkins and colleagues find that China represented only 2.5 percent of Argentine domestic manufacturing demand in 2006, yet a handful of industries saw the bulk of that demand. In seven manufacturing industries the share of Chinese imports in domestic demand increased by five percentage points between 2001 and 2006, and the share of domestic producers fell in six of those sectors. In four of those sectors, in the transport and electronics sectors, total demand increased (while China's increased and domestic producer share decreased), leading the authors to conclude that "China could be regarded as having had a negative impact on domestic production" (Jenkins 2009, 13). Jenkins also examines the impacts in Brazil, and finds that only two industries, lamps and lighting, and basic electronics, saw domestic contraction due to Chinese import penetration. With respect to employment, López and Ramos conclude that increased imports from

China have negatively affected employment levels in Argentina. Similar impacts on employment have been found in Chile (Álvarez and Claro 2009; López and Ramos 2007).

Conclusion

The findings in this chapter are stark and troubling. The analyses we conduct in this chapter shows that LAC manufacturing industries are increasingly being outcompeted by China in both the world and in regional LAC markets. Recent work on export similarity indices shows that this may only be the beginning. Rather than aiding in the diversification of LAC production and exports, China seems to be accentuating the narrowing of LAC production that has been occurring since the 1980s in the region. This is happening on two levels. On the one hand, as we showed in Chapter 2, Chinese demand and the secondary effect of that demand on world prices are increasing overall demand for LAC primary commodities in a few LAC countries. On the other, China is increasingly threatening LAC manufacturing exports in world and regional export markets. Indeed, this chapter shows that in world markets, over 94 percent of LAC manufactures exports are under some sort of threat from China, representing 40 percent of total exports. For Mexico the situation is even more grave, with 99 percent of manufacturing exports under threat, comprising 72 percent of total exports. The real jewel of an export economy, however, is in high-technology goods. The next chapter disaggregates the high-tech story in great detail.

4   Taking Away the Ladder?
The Fate of High-Tech Exports

Diversification is essential for the economic growth of nations, but the jewel of diversification is high-technology manufacturing because of its sheer dynamism and potential for significant economy-wide effects. To what extent are Latin American countries becoming more or less competitive in the global market for high-technology products? How does Latin America's performance compare with China's? Are LAC's high-tech exports "under threat"? This chapter accentuates the findings of the last: China is increasing its competitiveness in high-technology exports at an even greater speed than in manufactures as a whole.

Among a wide range of otherwise very different theoretical economic approaches, an underlying consensus exists about the importance of technological upgrading for sustainable economic growth and development. Moreover, empirical studies have shown that the technological sophistication of a country's exports is an important predictor of future growth. The question of whether LAC's high-technology exports are becoming more or less competitive is, therefore, critical for understanding the effects of recent policies in the region, as well as for informing a debate about future policy.

Our analysis is based on a detailed look at the evolution of both LAC's and China's competitiveness in global high-technology markets. We look at the evolution of shares of global exports for the eighteen sectors that have been classified in the literature as "high tech" at the three-digit level of the standard international trade classification (SITC) between 1985 and 2006. Once again, our core analytical concept is called dynamic revealed competitive position (DRCP), which we use to track the evolution of LAC and China's competitiveness in high-tech markets. In addition to looking at the region as a whole, we focus on a subset of countries that are particularly interesting in terms of their industrial capacities, and where technological development has played an important role in their development strategy (see the technical appendices for a detailed discussion of DRCP calculations).

The core finding of the chapter is that the competitiveness of LAC in high tech is stagnating or rapidly deteriorating for an overwhelming majority of high-tech products, which in many countries represent a significant share of aggregate exports. This finding is particularly striking in comparison with China's impressive performance in the opposite direction.

The chapter is organized as follows. First we present the theoretical and empirical arguments on technological upgrading and development. We then review the literature on the matter. We end by performing a series of analyses on high-technology manufacturing and conduct preliminary explorations into the realm of services trade.

Theoretical Perspectives on Trade, Technology, and Development

To what extent is the quality of a country's production and export basket a relevant dimension in the pursuit of economic development? This is a question that has drawn the interest of economists for centuries, and around which a rich body of both theoretical and empirical literature has developed. It is interesting to note that virtually all of the current "schools" of economic thought (except perhaps neo-Marxism) have stressed the importance of increasing the technological sophistication of a country's production and export basket, understood as climbing the technological ladder, in the pursuit of economic development. This short and far-from-exhaustive review simply demonstrates that technological upgrading is considered across the spectrum a key component of sustainable economic growth and development.

Neoclassical trade theory has developed around the Heckscher-Ohlin framework. Based on this theory, neoclassical economists have long argued that the income-maximizing strategy for a country is to export the goods in which it has a comparative advantage. Because technological diffusion is assumed to be instantaneous and costless, a country's comparative advantage is argued to be solely determined by its "fundamentals," that is, its factor endowments (the comparative advantage of a country is warranted to lie in the goods intensively produced using a country's relatively abundant production factor). In this sense, standard trade theory is neutral in terms of the technological composition of a country's export basket, as there is no built-in advantage to specializing in physical or human capital–intensive goods. However, even within the restrictive assumptions of Heckscher-Ohlin models, technological "upgrading" of a country's exports can take place. Within Heckscher-Ohlin trade theory, it is possible, through an exogenous change in factor endowments (brought about, for example, by foreign direct investment), for a country to diversify into trading more capital-intensive goods. Technically speaking, in the Heckscher-Ohlin framework this would mean that the factor endowment moves from outside to inside the "cone of diversification" (Jones 1987).

Staying within the boundaries of neoclassical economics but looking at the intertemporal welfare effects of trade patterns, Redding theoretically proves, using a general equilibrium model of endogenous growth and international trade between two large economies, that in some situations developing countries "face a trade-off between specializing according to an existing pattern of comparative advantage (often in low technology industries), and entering sectors where they currently lack a comparative advantage but may acquire such an advantage in the future as a result of the potential for productivity growth (e.g. high technology industries) (1999, 16)." Moreover, Redding argues,

> selective trade and industrial policies to induce specialization in sectors where an economy currently lacks a comparative advantage, but exhibits a large potential for productivity growth relative to its trading partner, may be welfare improving for the economy that imposes them. A lower initial level of instantaneous utility (resulting from specializing in a sector where no initial comparative advantage exists) may be more than offset by a higher rate of growth of instantaneous utility so that intertemporal welfare rises." (Redding 1999, 36).

Alternatively, some economists have argued that relaxing the assumption of costless technological diffusion in traditional (Heckscher-Ohlin) trade theory changes the outlook significantly. Theoretically, if technological diffusion is not costless, then the technological content of a country's production (and hence, trade pattern) becomes relevant. This is the case because technologically intensive structures have larger spillover effects in terms of creating new skills and generic knowledge that can be used in other activities. This suggests that in the absence of successful interventions to correct this market failure, countries are likely to be trapped in their technological level (Hausmann, Hwang, and Rodrik 2005; Lall 2000). As Lall, among others, has argued: "Technology intensive structures offer better prospects for future growth because their products tend to grow faster in trade: they tend to be highly income inelastic, create new demand, and substitute faster for older products" (2000, 339)—in addition, thanks to higher productivity levels, to being less vulnerable to competition from low-wage countries (Lall 2000).

A different variant of this approach is the "new" strategic trade theorists. A classic work by Grossman and Helpman (1991) shows that trade increases the technological capacity of a nation by transferring technological information, expanding the market, and thus spurring technological innovation. Evolutionary economists see technological change and innovation as the core of growth, and trade as no exception (Nelson and Winter 1982). Extensions of their theories of trade hold that international competitiveness is indeed a function of microlevel innovations in technology and increasing technological sophistication (Dosi and Soete 1983).

A different theoretical outlook on this issue was advanced in the late 1950s and 1960s by Raul Prebisch and his intellectual followers, and has come to be known as "structuralism." Prebisch's analysis began with the assumption, widely accepted, that the relative size of the primary sector tends to decline during the growth process, as a result of the low-income elasticity of demand for unprocessed agricultural goods, the substitution of raw materials for synthetic ones, and the increasing efficiency in the production of primary goods. Prebisch observed that because, for historical reasons, developed countries provide manufactured goods while developing countries (the "periphery") supply raw materials, the changes in productive structures brought about by economic growth generate a systemic bias against developing countries. The contraction in the relative size of primary activities affects less-developed countries more than proportionally.

This problem, argued Prebisch, is particularly trying because the redeployment of displaced workers to dynamic economic sectors faces several obstacles. First, there are political restrictions to the international migration of workers. Second, late industrializers face significant challenges in developing an industrial sector, associated with the great disparities in technology and capital availability with respect to the leading industrial centers.

> According to Prebisch, if workers displaced from primary sectors in the periphery are not adequately absorbed, labor incomes tend to fall. Simultaneously, workers in central countries are able to raise their incomes during business upswings and protect them during world recessions. Thus, the reduction in the relative size of the primary sector generated by a dynamic world economy tends to depress relative wages in the periphery. The adverse movement in relative wages tends to deteriorate, in turn, the terms of trade of developing countries. Evidently, relative international prices depend also on labor productivity in export activities. In Prebisch's view, however, the joint effect of the trends in wages and productivities implies that, whereas central countries are able to retain productivity improvement through higher real wages, those of the periphery are forced to "export" technological change through a deterioration in the factorial terms of trade (relative prices adjusted by productivity). (Ocampo 1993)

According to this structuralist argument, then, the export basket of a country is indeed relevant to its economic growth. The analysis, however, is conducted essentially in terms of primary products and manufacturing and not strictly in terms of technological levels. However, it is clear that the underlying logic of the structuralist argument would apply with even greater relevance to high-tech products, given the higher income elasticity of the demand for those products.

In sum, most theoretical perspectives—independently of their widely diverse assumptions—agree on the fact that technological upgrading is a critical element of sustainable economic growth.

Latin America and the Growth of China

As we have stressed throughout this book, across the world there is increasing concern about the effects of China's emergence on the global economic stage, and Latin America is no exception. As a result,

What is the structuralist arg?

among international organizations, academia, and government a burgeoning literature has emerged that attempts to examine the extent to which such concerns are justified.

We discuss these studies in great detail elsewhere in the volume (Blázquez-Lidoy, Rodríguez, and Santiso 2006; Devlin, Estevadeordal, and Rodriguez-Clare 2006; Dussel Peters 2005; Gottschalk and Prates 2005; Lall and Weiss 2005; Lederman, Olarreaga, and Perry 2009; Mesquita Moreira 2007; Paus 2009). In general, they look at the effects of China's growth in Latin America along three dimensions: bilateral trade, competition in third markets, and attraction of foreign direct investment.[1]

∴ However, these studies—with the exception of articles by Mesquita Moreira and Paus cited above—do not look at the issue of China's growth from a technological sophistication perspective. That is what we do in this chapter.

Analysis

In this section we compare the competitiveness of Latin America's high-technology exports in the world economy between 1985 and 2006 with those of China. More specifically, we demonstrate that the developed countries have lost considerable high-technology market share to the developing world and that, among developing countries, China has captured the majority of those gains. Then we compare LAC and selected countries with China's advancement.

Table 4.1 exhibits developed-country shares of global exports in 1985 and 2006 by technology level (for a discussion of the technology indices used in this analysis, see the technical appendix), along with the DRCP for each technology over that time period. The overall change over this period has been fairly dramatic, with the developed countries losing on average twenty percentage points of all global markets. Perhaps surprisingly, however, these changes are most profound in the high-technology sectors. Whereas in 1985 nearly 90 percent of global high-technology goods were produced and sold from developed countries, in 2006 developed-country high-technology exports were 56.8 percent of world high-technology exports—with a negative DRCP of 33.4.

However, as it had been the case for manufacturing as a whole, the reductions in market share for certain countries and regions in the

TABLE 4.1   Developed Countries Losing High-Tech Market Share

	Developed Country Share		
Tech Level	1985%	2006%	85-06 DRCP
PP	64.6	50.2	−14.4
RB	78.3	62.6	−15.7
LT	75.5	50.3	−25.3
MT	91.5	71.2	−20.3
HT	90.2	56.8	−33.4
Other	87.5	76.7	−10.7

NOTE: PP=primary product; RB=resource-based; LT=low technology; MT=medium
    technology; HT=high-technology
SOURCE: Authors' calculations based on United Nations Statistics Division (2009).

global high-tech export market take place in an expanding market. While
the expansion of the manufacturing export market had indeed been impressive (an expansion of 674% between 1985 and 2006), the expansion
in the high-tech market has been even more notable. Between 1985 and
2006, exports of high-tech products expanded more than tenfold, 1019
percent, by more than $2 trillion. As had been the case in the manufac-
turing market, within the overall growth in high-tech exports both Chinese and Latin American manufacturing exports grew significantly, albeit
in completely different orders of magnitude. Chinese high-technology manufacturing exports grew more than 100,000 percent between 1985 and
2006, while Latin American high-tech exports grew almost 2,500 percent, that is, by a factor of almost 25. Part of this difference, of course, is
explained by the fact that in 1985 Latin American high-tech exports were
significantly higher in number than Chinese exports. While Latin America
exported more than 3 billion, China only exported more than 300 million. However, that is only part of the picture.

In the context of growing a high-tech export market (in 1985
global high-technology exports stood at $400 billion and increased by
close to a factor of six in real terms by 2006 to over $2.5 trillion),
China's dramatic improvement is the direct result of the fact that China
captured the largest share of the market's growth (in other words, China
is the nation that best capitalized on the growth of the global high-tech
market). According to our calculations, the EU15 captured the greatest

share of the growth of high-tech exports with almost 30 percent (of which 11.29 percent is growth captured by Germany). China comes in second and captured 27.44 percent of the more than 200 million in growth in high-tech manufacturing exports between 2000 and 2006. It was the largest growth captured by a single country and represented more than all the growth captured by East Asia and the Pacific (including Japan), which captured 20.62 percent. The United States gained 3.78 percent. Latin America, as a whole, saw 2.21 percent of the growth, of which almost all was captured by Mexico (1.69 percent), while Brazil captured almost 0.4 percent.

As we will see later in the volume, perhaps even more impressive is how China has transformed its manufacturing base into one that is significantly composed of high-tech exports—and not just the lower rungs of the high-technology ladder.

The importance of high-tech products in the overall manufacturing export market has increased significantly. At the global level, the percentage of high-tech exports has increased on average in the world economy from 22 to 32 percent of total manufactures exports. This has also been the case with China's exports, albeit in a much more accelerated manner. In 1990 China's high-tech exports were a mere 10 percent of total manufacturing exports. By 2006 China's high tech share was approaching 40 percent of its total manufactures exports. Mexico nudged above the world average in 1996, but reached a plateau by 2000 at around 35 percent.

Focusing on competitiveness, table 4.2 looks at different countries' market shares in the global high-tech export market—as measured by the share of a nation's high-tech exports to total global high-tech manufacturing exports. In this table we examine how China and different LAC nations' competitiveness has improved in high-tech exports from 1985 to 2006. In terms of relative competitiveness, a quick look at the evolution of China's competitive position in comparative perspective highlights how dramatic China's gains in manufacturing competitiveness have been:

Table 4.2 literally shows how China is "climbing up the ladder" in global high-technology exports. This table exhibits global market shares in high-technology exports by country from 1985 to 2006, listing the top 30 for each year. In 1985 China was in twenty-ninth place

TABLE 4.2 Percentage of High-Tech Exports

1985	1990	1995	2000	2005
USA 25.3	USA 22.3	USA 16.1	USA 18.7	**China** **13.7**
Japan 17.3	Japan 16.1	Japan 15.2	Japan 10.7	USA 12.5
Fmr Fed. Rep. of Germany 11.5	Fmr Fed. Rep. of Germany 11.6	Germany 8.8	Germany 7.4	Germany 9.0
United Kingdom 8.5	United Kingdom 7.5	Singapore 6.9	Singapore 5.8	Japan 6.2
France 6.8	France 6.6	United Kingdom 5.8	United Kingdom 6.5	China, Hong Kong SAR 5.9
Italy 3.6	Italy 4.0	France 5.8	France 5.0	Singapore 5.7
Netherlands 3.3	Netherlands 3.6	China, Hong Kong SAR 4.2	China, Hong Kong SAR 4.5	United Kingdom 5.3
Canada 3.0	China, Hong Kong SAR 3.5	Rep. of Korea 4.2	Rep. of Korea 4.4	Rep. of Korea 4.7
China, Hong Kong SAR 2.3	Rep. of Korea 2.9	Netherlands 3.5	**China** **4.0**	France 4.4
Singapore 2.2	Switzerland 2.8	Malaysia 3.3	Malaysia 3.7	Netherlands 3.9
Switzerland 2.2	Canada 2.2	Italy 2.5	Netherlands 3.7	Malaysia 3.0
Sweden 1.9	Sweden 2.2	**China** **2.1**	Mexico 3.4	Mexico 2.7
Rep. of Korea 1.8	Belgium-Luxembourg 1.8	Canada 2.1	Canada 2.5	Belgium 2.5
Belgium-Luxembourg 1.6	Malaysia 1.6	Mexico 1.8	Ireland 2.3	Switzerland 1.8
Ireland 1.3	Ireland 1.6	Switzerland 1.8	Italy 2.0	Ireland 1.8
Malaysia 1.1	Austria 1.4	Sweden 1.7	Philippines 1.8	Italy 1.7
Denmark 0.8	Spain 1.1	Ireland 1.6	Sweden 1.7	Canada 1.6
Austria 0.7		Thailand 1.5	Belgium 1.5	Thailand 1.4

(*Continued*)

TABLE 4.2 (*Continued*)

1985		1990		1995		2000		2005	
Spain	0.7	Denmark	0.9	Belgium-Luxembourg	1.5	Thailand	1.5	Sweden	1.3
Poland	0.5	Thailand	0.7	Spain	0.9	Switzerland	1.4	Philippines	1.2
Israel	0.5	China	0.7	Finland	0.8	Finland	1.0	Spain	1.0
Czechoslovakia	0.4	Finland	0.5	Denmark	0.7	Spain	0.6	Hungary	0.9
Brazil	0.4	Israel	0.4	Austria	0.6	Israel	0.7	Austria	0.8
Finland	0.4	Australia	0.3	Australia	0.4	Austria	0.5	Finland	0.8
Norway	0.3	Norway	0.3	Israel	0.4	Denmark	0.6	Denmark	0.7
Australia	0.3	Brazil	0.3	Philippines	0.3	Hungary	0.6	Czech Rep.	0.7
Portugal	0.2	Czechoslovakia	0.3	Norway	0.3	Indonesia	0.5	Brazil	0.4
Hungary	0.2	Fmr Yugoslavia	0.2	Czech Rep.	0.2	Brazil	0.5	Israel	0.4
China	0.1	Mexico	0.2	Indonesia	0.2	Australia	0.3	Poland	0.4
Philippines	0.1	Poland	0.2	Brazil	0.2	Russian Federation	0.3	Indonesia	0.3

SOURCE: Authors' calculations based on United Nations Statistics Division (2009).

among high-technology exporters. By 2006 China ranked first with 13.7 percent of the global high tech market. The most stunning change is between 2000 and 2006—before and after China's entry into the World Trade Organization (WTO)—where China's DRCP was 9.7, far and away the largest increase in the entire period. However, China's market share at least doubles every five years beginning in 1985.

Only three Latin American nations enter the top 30 at any point since 1985, Argentina, Brazil, and Mexico. In 1985 Brazil ranked twenty-third and represented 0.4 percent of global high tech, and has more or less held that percentage of the market since. Mexico has a fairly impressive trajectory. Mexico did not find itself in the top thirty until 1990, sneaking in at number twenty-nine and 0.2 percent of the world market. It reached number twelve in the year 2000 and held 3.4 percent of global markets It remained in that place in 2006, although it lost market share—holding 2.7 percent of the market.

With 13.7 percent of the global high-tech market and a DRCP of 9.7 for the 2000–2006 period, China's performance in world high-tech markets is unrivaled. The only other noticeable changes are East Asia and Pacific (EAP) countries aside from China, which enter the picture in 1990 and together command almost 16 percent of global markets in 2006.

Latin America, driven by Mexico, also can be seen in the top thirty beginning in 1995. For 2006, China's exports of high technology were roughly $480 billion, and Latin America's stood at $80 billion. These figures are up from $140 billion and $70 billion respectively in 2000—a 238 percent increase by China and an 18 percent increase by LAC.

In terms of threat, since China's entry into the WTO it has been directly threatening all of the large LAC countries, with significant high-tech manufacturing sectors except for Colombia. Looking at the longer-term trend from 1985 to 2006 (column 1 in table 4.3), most of the region seems to be under only a partial threat, except for Argentina, which suffers a direct threat. China's DRCP is 13.58, and all of the LAC nations exhibited were below 1 percentage point (except Mexico, which has a DRCP of 1.82). Looking more recently, during the period 2000 to 2006 all countries except Colombia are directly threatened in high-technology exports. China's gain is 9.72 percentage points, while LAC as a whole and each of the specific countries have lost market share. While China's performance has been impressive for the whole period, the competitiveness

TABLE 4.3 China's Revealed Competitive Position: DRCP of China vs. Select Latin American Countries in High-Tech

	1985–2006 DRCP	1995–2006 DRCP	2000–2006 DRCP
Argentina	−0.03	0.00	−0.01
Brazil	0.03	0.27	−0.05
Chile	0.01	0.00	−0.001
Colombia	0.01	0.01	0.00
Costa Rica*	0.08	0.09	−0.05
Mexico*	1.82	0.87	−0.69
LAC	2.73	1.22	−0.81
China (Country)	13.58	11.60	9.72
China (Region)	17.19	13.26	11.15

*Data for 1985 was unavailable; 1985 calculation was performed with 1986 data.
SOURCE: Authors' calculations based on United Nations Statistics Division (2009).

of its high-tech exports (and overall manufacturing exports as well, as we saw in Chapter 3) took off in 2001, with China's entry into the WTO.

More than 95 percent of all LAC high-technology exports are under some type of threat from China, the majority of which are direct threats. In 2006, these threatened high-technology exports represented almost 12 percent of all LAC exports. Table 4.4 presents our calculations of the total volume of exports under threat from China between 2000 and 2006 as a percent of total high-technology exports and as a percent of total exports for LAC and our selection of countries in 2005.

Mexico, the one country in LAC that has made the greatest competitiveness progress over the entire 1985–2006 period, is also significantly threatened in the 2000–2006 period. Between 2000 and 2006, 65 percent of Mexico's high-technology exports were under direct threat, amounting to 32 percent of all of Mexico's exports. 16.6 percent of Mexico's high-technology exports are under partial threat and represent 8.2 percent of total exports. Combined, 82 percent of Mexico's high-technology exports are under some sort of threat from China, comprising of 40.1 percent of all Mexican exports.

However, Brazil and Costa Rica are the countries most threatened by China, with 96.7 percent of Brazil's high-technology exports, representing 7.2 percent of all of Brazil's exports in 2006, under some threat. In Costa Rica, 93.1 percent of its high-tech exports are under threat, rep-

TABLE 4.4   Percent of 2006 High-Tech and Total Exports Under Threat from China (2000–2006)

	Direct	Partial	Total
Argentina			
As % of HT exports in 2006	49.45	6.69	56.14
As % of all exports in 2006	1.21	0.16	1.37
Brazil			
As % of HT exports in 2006	41.24	52.42	93.66
As % of all exports in 2006	3.16	4.02	7.18
Chile			
As % of HT exports in 2006	0.13	0.07	0.2
As % of all exports in 2006	0.05	0.03	0.08
Colombia			
As % of HT exports in 2006	10.9	38.53	49.43
As % of all exports in 2006	0.26	0.92	1.18
Costa Rica			
As % of HT exports in 2006	31.57	61.53	93.1
As % of all exports in 2006	9.96	19.42	29.38
Mexico			
As % of HT exports in 2006	65.1	16.55	81.65
As % of all exports in 2006	32.3	8.21	40.51
LAC			
As % of HT exports in 2006	68.7	26.66	95.36
As % of all exports in 2006	8.28	3.21	11.49

SOURCE: Authors' calculations based on United Nations Statistics Division (2009).

resenting almost 30 percent of the country's exports. For Argentina and Colombia, more or less half of all high-technology exports are under threat, but in neither case do such exports represent over 2 percent of total exports.

China and the High-Tech Hurdle: Solely About Fragmentation?

In this section of the chapter, we show that, contrary to widespread beliefs, China's gain is not simply about fragmentation. Although a large share of its high-technology exports are indeed in final assembly, *what is fragmentation?*

China is increasingly diversifying its high-tech exports into more value-added activities. Here we formulate a data-driven examination of fragmentation and technological upgrading in Chinese and Mexican high-tech exports to shed light on this trait.

It is a fact that global production has become increasingly more fragmented (Gareffi, Humphrey, and Sturgeon 2005). Fragmentation poses challenges to traditional statistics and classifications of commodities such as the one we use in this chapter. In a world where a developing country can import parts of a device classified as "high tech," assemble it in a labor-intensive production facility, and then export it as a final "high-tech" product, export profiles organized along technological lines can be misleading.

For example, Lall, Weiss, and Zhang argue eloquently in a recent paper:

This is with the criticism I had

> Trade fragmentation weakens the link between core technical characteristics and production processes: some of the largest exporters of hi-tech electronics are low wage countries that only assemble and test final products (advanced design and component manufacture remains in rich countries). As a result, classifying semiconductors as high technology leads to the result that the Philippines has a more technology-intensive export structure than the US or Japan (Lall, 2000). The normal assumption that products use the same technologies across countries no longer holds when discrete processes can be separated. Moreover, "fragmentability" varies by activity. Within the hi-tech group, for instance, electronics is highly fragmentable (nearly 45 percent of world electronics exports come from developing countries) while aircraft or pharmaceuticals are not (their exports remain largely the preserve of rich countries). Gauging the real technological content of national exports would require data by process rather than product, but such data are simply not available. (Lall, Weiss, and Zhang 2005, 4)

Lall et al. have attempted to find a way around this problem and proposed a methodology to get at the heart of important product characteristics. As a complementary measure to the technological classification of exports, they propose a measure of sophistication that, for any given year and any given commodity, is a "weighted average (the weights being each country's shares of world exports) of exporters income" (2005, 7).

A similar approach is undertaken by Hausmann, Hwang, and Rodrik (2005), who construct an income/productivity index called *EXPY* for different countries' export baskets by taking a weighted average of the per-capita GDPs of the countries exporting a product, where the weights reflect the revealed comparative advantage of each country in that product.

Both approaches are an important contribution to the understanding of export sophistication. However, by organizing the analysis around the income of major exporters of any given product, they shift the focus away from technological characteristics to similarities to the export profiles of high-income countries. For large cross-country analyses, such an approach can be quite appropriate, even though it is likely that some anomalies will turn up. For instance, in both measures, Mexico turns out to have a relatively high level of technological sophistication, when in fact Mexican high-tech exports are highly concentrated in final assembly operations (Gallagher and Zarsky 2007). Since we are looking at a smaller number of countries and have the time to bore deeply into the data, we build on previous methodologies to obtain a more specific measure.

Using actual trade data provides a window through which to estimate when technological exports are the mere result of fragmentation and when actual upgrading of technological exports is taking place in an exporting country.

Our starting point is the eighteen products classified as high-tech by Lall (2000). Then, delving deeper into the trade data (sometimes getting to the five-digit level in the SITC classification), we gather information for final products as well as for the parts that go into the production of those final products.

Following this approach, we construct four distinct categories of products, chosen by both their propensity to be assembled in different locations (Amsden 2001) and the availability of deeper trade data at the input and final-product level. These sectors are: (1) office machines and automatic data-processing machines and units thereof; (2) electrical line telephonic and telegraphic apparatus; (3) microphones, loud-speakers, and audio-frequency electric amplifiers; (4) television receivers, radio-broadcast receivers; television, radio-broadcasting; transmitters; and telecommunications equipment. For the sake of brevity, we will refer to these as (1) computers, (2) telephones, (3) audio equipment, and (4) televisions and telecom.

The methodology we use for this chapter looks at net imports of parts and net imports of final products within each of the four categories

TABLE 4.5   Parts and Final Products for Selected High-Tech Manufactures

Category	Product		Parts	
	Code	Name	Code	Name
Computers	751	Office machines		
	752	Automatic data processing machines and units thereof	759	Parts of and accessories for machines of headings 751 or 752
Telephones	7641	Electrical line telephonic and telegraphic apparatus	76491	Parts of the apparatus falling within heading 7641
Audio equipment	7642	Microphones, loudspeakers, audio-frequency electric amplifiers	76492	Parts of the apparatus, equipment falling within heading 7642
Television and telecom	761	Television receivers		
	762	Radio-broadcast receivers		
	7643	Television, radio-broadcasting, transmitters, etc.		
	7648	Telecommunications equipment	76498	Parts of the apparatus of the headings 761, 762, 7643, and 7648

SOURCE: United Nations Statistics Division (2009).

of products. We look at net values to isolate, as much as possible, imports of parts and final products aimed at domestic consumption. We also look at the parts-to-final-products ratio (PFR), dividing the net exports of parts by the net exports of final product as a way to gauge the relative importance of part production and final-product production (see equation):

$$PFR = \frac{\sum_{Parts} X - \sum_{Parts} M}{\sum_{Final} X - \sum_{Final} M}$$

We look at the four possible combinations that can result from this analysis, as summarized in the following figure.

		Net exports of final products	
		+	**–**
Net export of parts	**+**	Net HT exporter	Outsourcer
	–	Assembler	Net HT importer

FIGURE 4.1   Framework for Value-Added Analysis

A positive sign results from a greater level of exports than imports; hence positive signs are corresponded with net export situations. To the contrary, a negative sign results from a greater level of imports than exports; hence negative signs are corresponded with net import situations. We label countries that are both net exporters (importers) of parts and final products as "net HT [high-tech] exporters" (net HT importers).

In turn, the scenarios where countries are both net exporters and net importers are particularly interesting and deserve closer attention. We argue that a country that is a net exporter of final products and a net importer of parts *within the same category* is likely to be reexporting those parts as final products. This is the economic phenomenon we refer to as assembly, and, for that reason, we classify countries where this combination is observed as "assemblers." The opposite case is that of a country that is a net exporter of parts and a net importer of final products *within the same category*. We argue that it is likely that in this case we are observing the flipside of the assembly story. Countries where this combination is observed are likely to be exporting parts and reimporting the final products, or outsourcing assembly activities. For that reason, we label countries in this category "outsourcers." In terms of Lall et al.'s argument, "real" technological content is related to research and development and not to assembly (Lall, Weiss, and Zhang 2005). Therefore, outsourcer countries are likely to have greater technological capacity than assemblers.

The evolution of the parts to final products ratio also captures some important information in terms of the path a country is undertaking. For example, an increase in the PFR in the case of an outsourcer would indicate that accentuation of the country's profile as an exporter of parts and importer of final products, a scenario that generally results from further developing domestic technological capacity.

The results of a close comparison between Mexico and China in all these dimensions are telling. We look only at the case of Mexico in Latin America because, as it is clear from table 4.2, Mexico is the only country that has achieved and retained a level of high-tech competitiveness in global markets (Mexico is the only LAC country to even rank in the top twenty high-tech exporters).

Table 4.6 shows that between 2000 and 2006, Mexico went from being a net HT exporter to an "assembler in one sector (computers) and from an Outsourcer to an Assembler in another (television and telecom). While Mexico appears to have held its ground in telephones, the opposite is true in audio equipment (between 2000 and 2006, when Mexico remained an assembler, imports of parts increased).

China, on the other hand, held its ground in all four sectors. In computers, in which China remained a net HT exporter, the ratio of parts to final products increased significantly, signaling that China may be well on its way to becoming an outsourcer. On the other hand, in audio equipment, China's characteristics as an assembler remained relatively constant, as net imports of parts increased proportionally at the same rate as net exports of final products. Like the other methodologies, our depiction is far from perfect—but it is consistent with the literature. Indeed, this transformation is supported by other literature that shows how China is now beginning to export final products under its own brands such as Lenovo and is domestically manufacturing high volumes of parts rather than importing them (Fan and Watanabe 2006). Rodrik, using the *EXPY* analysis discussed above came to similar conclusions for the high-tech sector (Rodrik 2006). He finds that "a strong domestic producer base has been important in diffusing imported technology and in creating domestic supply chains." Indeed, foreign assembly plans are a "rarity" now among the leaders in the industry. Most firms are joint ventures between foreign and domestic (mostly state-owned) firms. In the case of Mexico, more than 95 percent of all high-tech firms—and their suppliers—are foreign assembly plants (Gallagher and Zarsky 2007).

TABLE 4.6 Value-Added Analysis

		Mexico		China	
		2000	*2006*	*2000*	*2006*
Computers	NXP*	1,126	–2,164	111	14,426
	NXFP*	4,980	2,866	7,668	79,389
	PFR	23%	–76%	1%	18%
		Net HT Exporter	Assembler	Net HT Exporter	Net HT Exporter
Telephones	NXP	270	838	–1,343	–119
	NXFP	1,406	525	591	9,126
	PFR	19%	160%	–227%	–1%
		Net HT Exporter	Net HT Exporter	Assembler	Assembler
Audio equipment	NXP	–59	–151	–4	–14
	NXFP	471	189	954	2,906
	PFR	–13%	–80%	0%	0%
	PFR	Assembler	Assembler	Assembler	Assembler
Television and telecom	NXP	76	–7,220	7,837	20,248
	NXFP	–1,257	5,483	5,248	50,658
	PFR	–6%	–132%	149%	40%
		Out-sourcer	Assembler	Net HT Exporter	Net HT Exporter

*NXP and NXFP shown as millions of current dollars.
SOURCE: Authors' calculations based on United Nations Statistics Division (2009).

In sum, whereas Mexico and Latin America are falling down the ladder in terms of DRCP and shifting toward assembly, China is climbing up the ladder and developing its own flagship industries. The purpose of this section was to address the concern that in the context of international fragmentation of production, the link between core technical characteristics and production processes is significantly weakened. If this were to be the case, competitiveness in high-technology products would not necessarily be an encouraging development. While there is no question that theoretically this mismatch between competitiveness in high-technology and technological upgrading is a possibility, we believe that in practice, competitiveness in high-tech exports and real technological upgrading are empirically related. For example, nations such as Taiwan started with firms that were final assemblers of high-tech products and now have full-fledged companies (Amsden and Chu 2003).

Services to the Rescue?

Given that Latin America's competitiveness is falling behind both in manufacturing as a whole (see previous chapter) and in high tech specifically, it is worth asking how Latin America is faring in terms of competitiveness in services exports, and whether services could come to the "rescue" of Latin America in an otherwise bleak competitiveness outlook. First and foremost, however, it is important to stress that when compared to trade in goods, trade in services is still significantly less important, particularly for China and Latin America. Since 1985, trade in services has continuously represented around 20 percent of total trade for the world as a whole. However, for both China and Latin America, the relative importance of trade in services has been decreasing. In 1985 services exports were 11 percent of China's total exports but slid to 9 percent in 2006. Services comprised 21 percent of LAC exports in 1985 but only 12 percent by 2006.

To date, only one other study that we know of analyzes China's impact on LAC services exports. In an analysis that examines the relative competitiveness of China and India vis-à-vis LAC in the U.S. market, Caroline Freund of the World Bank found no evidence that these countries' services exports to the United States displaced LAC exports to that market. Moreover, Freund stresses that, as of 2004, services exports to the United States from LAC were still seven times greater than those of China and India, reflecting the importance of proximity, particularly in tourism (Freund 2009).

To address the question of whether services could come to the "rescue" of Latin America in an otherwise bleak competitiveness outlook, we mirror the analyses conducted in this and the previous chapter, but for exports of services. It is important to stress that data for services (and services exports in particular) are much less complete and comprehensive than data for trade in goods. There are plenty of holes in the data, in every database. Precisely because of these limitations, we conduct our analysis only at the greatest level of aggregation, that is, total exports of services. This is the level at which services data can be obtained with significant breadth. We use "Trade in services by service-category and country" data from UNCTAD's 2008 *Handbook of Statistics* (UNCTAD 2009). We include India in our analysis because it has been widely mentioned in the literature as well as in the popular press as a country that is quickly becoming much more competitive in the services sector.

Just as had been the case with manufacturing in general and high tech in particular, exports of services grew significantly between 1985 and 2006, almost sixfold (599%). Exports of services by Latin America, China, and India also grew significantly in the period. China's and India's exports of services grew at a different level of magnitude from that of Latin America. While China's and India's services exports increased by almost a factor of 30 between 1985 and 2006 (2,911 and 2,127 percent respectively), Latin America's export of services increased more than threefold, 381 percent. As was the case with manufacturing and high tech, these differences are mainly explained by the fact that at the beginning of the period, Latin America exported significantly more than China and India in services. At the end of the period, India, and especially China, caught up. Actually, in 2006, China services exports were 7 percent greater than those of Latin America. However, in sharp contrast with the reality in general manufacturing and high-tech manufacturing, these differences matter less, because neither China nor India nor Latin America are significant players in the services export sector.

The majority of the growth in global services trade did not occur in China or LAC but in the United States, European Union, and East Asia and the Pacific (excluding China). We calculated the share of the total growth in services exports between 2000 and 2006 that were captured by China, India, and Latin America in comparative perspective. The EU15, East Asia and the Pacific (excluding China), and the United States captured almost 75 percent of all the growth, with Latin America, China, and India capturing much smaller shares at 3 percent, 4 percent, and 3 percent respectively.

Table 4.7 shows the "ladder" of services exports, that is, the ranking of countries with the greatest market shares of services exports between 1980 and 2006. Contrary to what had been the case with manufacturing and high-tech exports, OECD countries still dominate services exports. However, China and India have managed—particularly in the

TABLE 4.7 The Services Trade Ladder

1990 (%)		1995 (%)		2000 (%)		2005 (%)	
United States	17.7	United States	17.7	United States	19.4	United States	14.9
France	9.1	France	6.8	United Kingdom	7.9	United Kingdom	8.2
Germany	7.0	Germany	6.5	Germany	5.5	Germany	6.2
United Kingdom	6.8	United Kingdom	6.2	France	5.3	France	4.2
Italy	6.0	Japan	5.3	Japan	4.5	Japan	4.2
Japan	5.0	Italy	5.0	Italy	3.7	Spain	3.5
Netherlands	3.5	Netherlands	3.7	Spain	3.5	Italy	3.6
Belgium-Luxembourg	3.4	Spain	3.3	Belgium-Luxembourg	3.3	China	3.3
Spain	3.3	Belgium-Luxembourg	2.9	Netherlands	3.2	Netherlands	2.9
Austria	2.8	China, Hong Kong SAR	2.8	China, Hong Kong SAR	2.7	India	2.7
Switzerland	2.4	Austria	2.6	Canada	2.6	China, Hong Kong SAR	2.6
Canada	2.3	Switzerland	2.2	Austria	2.1	Ireland	2.5
China, Hong Kong SAR	2.2	Canada	2.1	Republic of Korea	2.0	Belgium	2.1
Sweden	1.7	Singapore	2.1	China	2.0	Canada	2.1
Denmark	1.6	Republic of Korea	1.9	Switzerland	2.0	Singapore	2.1
Singapore	1.5	China	1.6	Singapore	1.6	Denmark	1.9
Norway	1.5	Australia	1.3	Denmark	1.3	Switzerland	1.9
Greece	1.3	Sweden	1.3	Sweden	1.3	Republic of Korea	1.8
Australia	1.2	Denmark	1.2	China, Taiwan, Province of	1.2	Luxembourg	1.8

Republic of Korea		China, Taiwan, Province of		Australia		Sweden	
Republic of Korea	1.2	China, Taiwan, Province of	1.2	Australia	1.3	Sweden	1.8
Mexico	1.0	Thailand	1.2	Turkey	1.3	Austria	1.7
Turkey	1.0	Turkey	1.2	Greece	1.3	Greece	1.3
China, Taiwan, Province of	0.8	Norway	1.1	Norway	1.1	Norway	1.2
Thailand	0.8	Greece	1.0	Ireland	1.1	Australia	1.2
SFR of Yugoslavia (former)	0.8	Malaysia	0.9	India	1.1	Russian Federation	1.1
Egypt	0.7	Russian Federation	0.9	Israel	1.0	China, Taiwan, Province of	1.0
China	**0.7**	Philippines	0.8	Malaysia	0.9	Turkey	0.9
Portugal	0.6	Mexico	0.8	Thailand	0.9	Thailand	0.9
Finland	0.5	**Poland**	0.8	Mexico	0.9	Malaysia	0.8
India	0.6	Egypt	0.7	Poland	0.7	Poland	0.7
Israel	0.5	Portugal	0.7	Egypt	0.6	Brazil	0.7
Malaysia	0.5	Israel	0.6	Russian Federation	0.6	Israel	0.7
Brazil	0.4	Finland	0.6	Brazil	0.6	Portugal	0.6
South Africa	0.4	India	0.6	Portugal	0.6	Mexico	0.6
Ireland	0.4	Czech Republic	0.5	Finland	0.5	Egypt	0.6
Philippines	0.4	Brazil	0.5	Czech Republic	0.5	Finland	0.6
Poland	0.4	Indonesia	0.4	Hungary	0.4	Czech Republic	0.5
Saudi Arabia	0.4	Hungary	0.4	Indonesia	0.4	Hungary	0.5
Hungary	0.3	Ireland	0.4	South Africa	0.3	South Africa	0.4
Czechoslovakia (former)	0.3	South Africa	0.4	Argentina	0.3	Lebanon	0.4

(Continued)

TABLE 4.7 (*Continued*)

1990 (%)		1995 (%)		2000 (%)		2005 (%)	
Indonesia	0.3	Argentina	0.3	New Zealand	0.3	Ukraine	0.4
Argentina	0.3	Saudi Arabia	0.3	Chile	0.3	Croatia	0.4
Morocco	0.2	Cyprus	0.3	Croatia	0.3	China, Macao SAR	0.4
Cyprus	0.2	Chile	0.3	Cyprus	0.3	Morocco	0.4
Chile	0.2	China, Macao SAR	0.3	Ukraine	0.3	New Zealand	0.3
Tunisia	0.2	Ukraine	0.2	China, Macao SAR	0.2	Argentina	0.3
Colombia	0.2	Tunisia	0.2	Philippines	0.2	Chile	0.3
Bahamas	0.2	Croatia	0.2	Dominican Republic	0.2	Saudi Arabia	0.3
China, Macao SAR	0.2	Viet Nam	0.2	Cuba	0.2	Cyprus	0.3

SOURCE: Authors' elaboration based on UNCTAD (2009).

last couple of years—to sneak into the top ten services exporters, while the share of countries in Latin America (particularly Argentina, Brazil, and Mexico) has either decreased or remained constant.

Finally, in terms of "threat," we find that all countries in Latin America are under some sort of competitive threat from China and India. A small group of countries are under partial threat, but the vast majority are under direct threat (UNCTAD 2009).

Therefore, after this short analysis, it is hard to conclude that in the bleak competitive scenario we have described, services could come to the "rescue" of Latin America.

Conclusions and Suggestions for Further Research

China is rapidly becoming a leader in global high-technology markets. It is experiencing the fastest and most sustaining growth and is moving from assembly operations to more sophisticated types of high-technology exports. LAC is either lagging behind or, in the case of Mexico, barely standing in place. Moreover, Mexico remains a low-wage assembly haven for U.S. products and is not showing much of an increase in the sophistication of high-tech exports.

More specifically, in this chapter we calculated what we call the DRCP of nations for high-technology exports (and to some extent services) between 1985 and 2006. We find that the developed world has lost significant market share in high technology and that China has climbed the high-technology ladder during this period. In 1985 China was ranked twenty-ninth of all nations in terms of the percentage of global exports in high technology. By 2006 China had climbed to the first place in the world. This dramatic leap is due not only to fragmentation, but also to some significant upgrading of Chinese industry. We also find that close to 95 percent of all of LAC's exports are under some sort of "threat" from China, comprising almost 12 percent of total exports from LAC. This condition is most pronounced in Brazil and Costa Rica, where over 93 percent of all high-technology exports are under threat. In Costa Rica, such exports represent almost 30 percent of total exports. Most of these trends become very accentuated during the period 2000–2006, when one could almost make the case that China is "taking away the ladder" from LAC. It is hard to overstate the impact of this development for Latin

America and the Caribbean, as, for example, Cimoli and Katz have argued:

> The present pattern of production specialization—strongly biased in favor of industries featuring low domestic knowledge generation and value-added content—and the inhibition of local R&D and engineering activities resulting from the rapid expansion of internationally integrated production systems are pushing Latin American economies into a "low development trap." (Cimoli and Katz 2003)

The aim of this chapter has been to map the relative competitiveness trajectories occurring in the high-technology sector between China and LAC. Both of the previous chapters point to Mexico as the nation currently under the largest threat from China. For this reason, we devote the next two chapters to unpacking the China-Mexico economic relationship.

5   Clear and Present Danger

Mexico and China in the U.S. Market

Regardless of whether analysts have used an export structure approach or a dynamic one, Mexico stands out as being significantly outcompeted by Chinese firms in the world economy. For that reason we devote this and the next chapter to analyzing Mexico's plight in great detail. This chapter pinpoints the sectors that are under threat in Mexico's most important market—the United States. The next chapter compares economic policy in the two countries. This chapter has three parts. The first part outlines existing work on Mexico, part two presents our analysis of Mexico, and the third part summarizes our findings and raises key questions for the next chapter.

The Jury Is In: Mexico Is Out

Though some very early studies on Mexico did not see much of a problem, there is now near unanimous concern about Mexico's industrial competitiveness vis-à-vis China. Those studies that look at a period ending in 2001 or 2002 and that use early base years find that China is not much of a threat to Mexico. Those studies that include analyses of years following China's entry into the WTO in 2001 find that Mexico should be very concerned about its competitive position in the U.S. and world economy relative to China.

Devlin, Estevadeordal, and Rodriguez-Clare (2006) compare penetration to the U.S. manufacturing market in 1972 with 2001, with the aim of assessing the impact of China's export boom for Latin American exports. For this broad period, they find that the countries that experienced the greatest market share gain were first, China, and second, Mexico. The gain for China came from "miscellaneous manufacturing" and for Mexico from "machinery." They also look at the textile sector in more detail and find that since 1997 China has been an ever growing export force in the U.S. market.

Lall and Weiss (2005) put forward a more detailed analysis of the evolution the shares of Latin American (in general) and Mexican (in particular) import shares in both the U.S. and world markets. They assess the "competitive threat" posed by China to Latin America. They compare export structures to evaluate "potential for competition" and look at the evolution of China's shares in both the world and U.S. markets. Lall and Weiss research the period 1990–2002. They find that Mexico is not under significant threat by China, nor is Costa Rica, the other country with a competitive export structure. Indeed, for the period they study, they find that the positions of these countries improved. Working at the three-digit SITC level, they show that while in 1990 23.6 percent of Mexican exports to the United States were under some sort of threat, the percentage of exports in the same category in 2002 had decreased to 11.2 percent.

On the whole they find that Mexico was not becoming more threatened by China during this period. However, what a difference a few years make. A commentary of ours to the Lall and Weiss article published in the same journal and using the same methodology with only two new years of data showed the majority of Mexico's exports were under some type of "threat" (Gallagher and Porzecanski 2007).

An approach similar to Lall and Weiss's is adopted by Dussel Peters (2005), who looked at the top ten Mexican and Central American exports to the U.S. market in 2003. He analyzes the extent to which China poses a competitive threat based on the evolution of the importance of the U.S. market for their top ten exports (Dussel Peters 2005). He shows that Mexico's top ten exports to the U.S. market represent 83.77 percent of its exports. Those same products represent 52.27 percent of China's exports to the U.S., indicating a high potential for conflict. Moreover, Dussel Peters concludes that in light industrial sectors such as clothing and apparel, as well as in electronics, Mexico is beginning to experience threats from China. Dussel Peters predicts that other final assembly sectors would follow suit. A more recent study by Dussel

Peters that looks specifically at Mexico's personal computer industry came to even more grave conclusions. Dussel Peters finds that Mexico's market share in U.S. imports of personal computers went from 14 percent to 7 percent during the period 2001–2006, whereas China's share grew from 14 percent to 45 percent (Dussel Peters 2008b)

Recent work by Feenstra and Kee (2007) compares trade liberalization and the proliferation of export varieties in Mexico and China between 1990 and 2001. They find that Mexico on average exported 52 percent of all product varieties imported by the United States in 1990, and 67 percent in 2001—affirming the hypothesis that trade liberalization accelerates the proliferation of export variety. However, they also find that China had 42 percent of all U.S. product varieties in 1990 and 63 percent in 2001. Though China's overall percentage is still shy of Mexico's, it shows that China's proliferation of export varieties to the United States is growing faster and may be a threat to Mexican exports.

Finally, in two studies published in the journal *World Development*, Sargent and Matthews look at the impact of Chinese competition on Mexico's export processing zone industry (also known as *maquila*). In one study, they find that after China's entry into the WTO, Mexican maquilas across the spectrum (in terms of both technology and location) rely exclusively on proximity-dependent strategies. In other words, China may be forcing Mexican maquilas to cling to their last comparative advantage: geographic proximity to the U.S. market (Sargent and Matthews 2008). In a second study, Sargent and Matthews look more directly at the effect of Chinese competition in the U.S. market on maquila losses in Mexico, in search of any characteristic in Mexican maquilas that may shield them from Chinese competition. Their findings suggest that China's export surge has contributed to relatively high rates of maquila mortality in low-, medium-, and high-quality maquila segments. In other words, they find that Chinese competition is blind to the quality of the competing maquila. Sargent and Matthews do find, however, that larger maquilas and plants producing auto parts enjoyed lower mortality rates (2009).

Our Analysis of Mexico

When Mexico integrated with the U.S. economy, Mexicans thought being an export platform to the largest economy in the world would lead them on the road to riches. Now they fear that they are losing ground to China.

After decades of an inward-looking economic strategy, Mexico opened its doors to the global economy in the late 1980s to follow a strategy based on trade and investment liberalization. A key goal in this strategy has been to gain ever-increasing access to the largest market in the world—Mexico's northern neighbor, the United States. Liberalization began in the 1980s and culminated in the North American Free Trade Agreement, launched in 1994. The hope was that by transforming itself into an export-oriented economy with preferential access to the United States, Mexico would attract foreign and domestic investment to support long-term economic growth.

In terms of generating non-oil exports and increasing access to the U.S. economy, Mexico's plan was a success (in general, analyses of the performance of Mexican exports look at the non-oil sector to isolate from the analysis the effect of this sector with such unique characteristics) . The volume of non-oil exports has increased by a factor of 10 since 1980. Almost 90 percent of these non-oil exports are headed to the United States. In relation to the Mexican economy, exports formed only 10 percent of GDP in 1980 but stand at 30 percent today. Perhaps most successfully, the variety of exports increased. In 1980, 80 percent of all Mexican exports were from the oil sector, but today, oil accounts for only approximately 10 percent of total exports. The bulk of Mexico's manufactured exports are in the automotive, electronic, and textile sectors—the majority of the latter being produced by in-bond firms (maquiladoras). Finally, Mexico enjoys a large trade surplus with the United States.

Today, Mexicans are very concerned that they are losing ground to other developing countries, especially China. Between 2000 and 2006, U.S. imports grew 53 percent, from 1.26 to 1.92 trillion. Almost a third of that growth was captured by China (30%), followed by Canada (11.4%), Mexico (9.5%), and Germany (4.7%). China, which was not a significant trading partner until the mid-1990s, is now the United States' largest trading partner. China has leapt over Mexico's long-standing spot as the third largest exporter to the United States and displaced Canada as the largest source of United States imports (United Nations Statistics Division 2009).

While Mexico retains a large share of the U.S. market, its competitive position could erode. When the United States suffers, so does Mexico, as the U.S. market has become the linchpin of the Mexican economy. More than 85 percent of all Mexico's exports are destined for the United States. Moreover, 50 percent of all Mexican imports come from the United States (United Nations Statistics Division 2009).

Looking at the extent to which Mexico is becoming more or less competitive, we find that the fears of many Mexicans may be justified. Indeed, since China joined the World Trade Organization in 2001, over 80 percent of Mexico's exports to the United States are under some sort of "threat" from China.

We look at Mexico's top fifteen exports, as well as its most and least dynamic sectors. Finally, we also conduct this analysis by sorting Mexican exports to the U.S. economy by level of technology. This allows us to assess the extent to which Mexico is gaining ground in the U.S. economy relative to China by level of technology. As in other chapters in the volume, we deploy the technology classification system established by Lall (2000) that is elaborated on in the technical appendix.

In this section we present the calculations of DRCP for the entirety of Mexico's exports to the United States and examine two things: (1) the extent to which they are gaining more access to the U.S. market; and (2) the extent to which specific sectors are "threatened" by China. We find that as each year has progressed, especially since China's entry into the WTO, Mexican exports face an ever growing threat from China. Just a handful of sectors are keeping Mexico in its place as the third-largest exporter to the United States. We also identify the fifteen sectors that more rapidly penetrated the U.S. market.

Table 5.1 exhibits the percentage of Mexican exports to the United States threatened by China from 1985 to 2006, measured in the last year of the period. During the period 1985–1990, 41.9 percent of Mexican exports were under either direct or partial threat. By 2006 that figure was 80.3 percent (note that Chapter 3 finds that 99 percent of Mexico's exports to the world are threatened; this chapter looks solely at Mexico's most crucial market, the United States). It is also important to note that the vast majority of threatened sectors are classified as a "direct threat" after 2000. That measure stood at 12.3 percent during the 1985–1990

TABLE 5.1 Percentage of Mexican Exports Under "Threat" from China, 1985–2006*

	1985–1990	1990–1995	1995–2000	2000–2006
Direct threat	12.3	10.8	7.1	46.8
Partial threat	29.6	65.7	68.7	33.5
Total	41.9	76.5	75.8	80.3

SOURCE: Authors' calculation based on United Nations Statistics Division (2009).
*Percentage of Mexican Exports to the United States *in the Final Year of the Period* that are under threat from China in the U.S. market.

period, was as low as 7.1 percent during the period 1995–2000, but reached 46.8 percent between 2000 and 2006.

Mexico's Top 20 Exports

This section looks at the relative competitiveness of Mexico's top exports. We focus on Mexico's twenty largest non-oil export sectors destined for the United States, which comprised almost $140 billion, or 55 percent, of Mexico's exports to the United States in 2006. Moreover, Mexico enjoys a trade balance of $30 billion in these twenty products. In 2006 Mexico's top export to the United States was passenger cars, followed by television receivers, telecommunication equipment, auto parts, and electronics. Also among the top twenty were base metals, vegetables, and furniture products. Table 5.2 exhibits the DRCP of these top twenty exports.

During the period analyzed, we find that over 80 percent of Mexican exports are under "direct" or "partial" threat. In the industries that account for the largest bulk of Mexico's exports, Mexico did not register a major gain in the U.S. market, and some industries saw their share actually recede. Table 5.2 exhibits the DRCP for the top twenty exports and shows that although the share in the U.S. market increased for nine of the twenty sectors, on the whole there was a one-percentage-point non-weighted average decrease in the share of these top twenty sectors in the United States. China, in contrast, averaged a 10.9 percentage point gain in these same twenty sectors.

In only two sectors did Mexico's share in the U.S. market rise and China's diminish: refined petroleum products and medical instruments.

TABLE 5.2 DRCP for Mexico's 2006 Top 20 Non-oil Exports

Commodity	2006 Value	Mexico Share of U.S. Imports (%) 2000	2006	DRCP Mexico	China
Television receivers	15,016,561,273	62.6	50.6	-12.0	25.0
Passenger motor vehicles (excluding buses)	13,860,259,979	14.3	10.4	-3.9	0.2
Telecommunication equipment parts and accessories	11,163,561,296	20.3	13.5	-6.8	23.0
Motor vehicle parts and accessories	10,774,070,584	16.0	20.6	4.6	4.7
Trucks and special-purposes motor vehicles	8,059,830,305	31.6	43.5	11.9	0.0
Automatic data processing machines and units thereof	7,637,887,655	11.3	8.1	-3.1	38.9
Equipment for distribution of electricity	7,438,879,881	61.3	52.1	-9.2	7.4
Electrical machinery and apparatus	7,115,089,408	18.0	22.1	4.1	11.6
Electrical apparatus for making and breaking electrical circuits	5,877,304,989	23.9	27.3	3.4	8.9
Furniture and parts thereof	4,501,761,676	15.6	12.3	-3.3	22.5
Internal combustion piston engines, and parts thereof	4,199,233,856	16.8	20.1	3.2	1.7
Measuring, checking, analysis, controlling instruments, parts	3,522,047,789	15.4	12.5	-2.8	5.6
Manufactures of base metal	3,492,117,349	17.1	16.6	-0.5	17.0
Petroleum products, refined	3,246,576,603	2.8	4.2	1.4	-0.3
Medical instruments and appliances	2,833,009,420	20.3	23.9	3.6	-0.1
Rotating electric plant and parts thereof	2,595,345,697	32.3	23.8	-8.5	8.2
Nonelectric parts and accessories of machinery	2,569,664,770	13.1	10.2	-2.9	9.1
Household type equipment	2,335,445,172	16.7	20.7	4.0	8.5
Parts, nes of, and accessories for machines of headings 751 or 752	2,075,332,045	7.0	3.6	-3.4	24.0
Vegetables, fresh or simply preserved; roots and tubers	416,315,106	50.9	51.5	0.6	2.1

SOURCE: Authors' calculation based on United Nations Statistics Division (2009).

In other words, in these two sectors, Mexico poses a direct threat to China. Mexico also poses a partial threat to China in piston engines and trucks. These goods are heavier by nature and thus have higher transportation costs. In addition, NAFTA's rules of origin require that over 60 percent of transport vehicles sold in North America are manufactured in the region as well—acting like a local content standard.

In eleven sectors the Mexico rate of penetration of the U.S. market decreased and China's increased (direct threats). Among these are passenger motor vehicles, where Mexico lost 3.9 percentage points but China gained 0.2, and automatic data processing machines, or computers, where Mexico lost 3.1 percentage points but China gained 38.9. China's success in these industries is remarkable given that computers take eighteen hours to travel to the United States from Mexico, versus almost eighteen *days* by ship from China (Gallagher and Zarsky 2007). Clearly transportation costs have lost relevance in relation to other costs of production in this sector. In addition, during this period, China faced a tariff of six percent on goods entering the United States and Mexico's was zero, even after WTO entry for these products (Dussel Peters 2005).

One additional sector in which Mexico has clearly lost competitiveness is the television receiver industry. In the early 1980s practically no television receivers manufactured in Mexico were exported to the United States, but by 2000 Mexican television receivers covered more than 65 percent of the corresponding U.S. imports. Indeed, Lall and Weiss (2005) found that it was one of the sectors where Mexico was a threat to China in the U.S. market. However, from 2000 to 2006, Mexico saw a decrease in its share of 12.04 percentage points. During the same period, China's share increased by 25.02 percentage points.

These findings are consistent with the literature cited above that has looked at the post-2001 period. When taking into account the years following China's accession to the WTO (2001), by and large Mexico's key exports have either stagnated or are growing much slower than their Chinese counterparts. Those sectors that hold ground are low-skilled work-assembly operations with higher transportation costs.

Most and Least Dynamic Sectors

In addition to Mexico's most important exports, we analyze DRCP for all sectors of the Mexican economy, regardless of their overall importance to Mexico's export profile. Indeed we identify twenty sectors where Mexico is gaining the most ground in the U.S. economy, and the twenty sectors where Mexico is losing the most. Again we compare these gains and losses to China.

Interestingly, eleven of the twenty products that comprise the 20 most dynamic exports by Mexico to the U.S. market are primary products. Also interesting, however, is our finding that in all but three sectors, Mexico is a direct or partial threat to China.

We define a dynamic product as the product whose percentage as a share of total U.S. imports (as reported by the United States) increased the most between 2000 and 2006. These products represent 6.5 percent of Mexico's total exports. All of them have gained more than five percentage points of access into the United States, and some sectors like cereals, sugar and honey, and gold have gained more than fifteen percentage points. Of the top twenty, ten are in primary-product or resource-based sectors, and nine are in manufacturing. China is gaining share in all but five.

Only one sector, trucks, is among the top twenty Mexican exports analyzed earlier. Take that sector away, and these dynamic sectors comprise 3.1 percent of Mexico's exports to the world. This in itself may not be problematic. After all, it may just reflect the fact that once you reach a certain share of the U.S. import market, it is not possible to keep expanding it at an accelerated rate.

We also examine the twenty sectors where Mexico registers the largest reductions in its share of total imports in the U.S. market. In all of these twenty sectors, Mexico would be classified as under direct threat from China. The sectors most hit were railway vehicles, sulphur and unroasted iron pyrites, synthetic fibers for spinning, television receivers (already discussed above because it is such a large export), and garments.

With the exception of televisions, these sectors do not represent a major share of Mexican exports (they add up to 13.1% of Mexican exports, excluding TVs). However, they are an important share of U.S. imports in each sector. In 2000 Mexico supplied 30 percent of all U.S. imports of railway vehicles, 50 percent of all sulphur and iron pyrites, 16 percent of synthetic fibers, and 62 percent of all television receivers. We have already noted that televisions from Mexico are now down to 50 percent of total U.S. imports. Railway vehicles, however, are down to 8 percent of U.S. imports—a reduction of almost 22 percentage points from 2000. Fibers and garments are down thirteen and eleven percentage points respectively. In all these sectors, China has made significant gains in the U.S. market.

Competitiveness and Technological Development

As discussed in depth in the last chapter, developing countries hope that export openness and increased trade will result in their climbing the technological ladder, diversifying from primary-product and resource-based production toward higher-technology exports. Indeed, a recent economic study by Imbs and Wacziarg showed that as nations that develop, sectoral production and employment move from relatively high concentrations to diversity. They find that nations do not stabilize their diversity until they reach an average level of income of over $15,000 (Imbs and Wacziarg 2003).

Using the technological scale developed by Lall (see appendix), we find that since 1986 Mexico's export profile has indeed diversified away from primary-product (PP) and resource-based (RB) products. In 1986, 40.5 percent of Mexico's non-oil exports were PP and RB; by 2006 the two combined were less than 14 percent. The biggest growth has been in medium-technology (MT) and high-technology (HT) goods. In 1986, 46.8 percent of Mexican exports fell in these categories, but by 2006 MT and HT exports were 72 percent of the total.

Interestingly, however, the majority of diversification toward MT occurred before NAFTA. Needless to say, this evolution is contrary to the high expectations that were raised for Mexico's industry in the wake of NAFTA. Since NAFTA, the share of Mexican non-oil exports that are MT and LT has more or less stagnated. A similar thing happened with HT. While the share of HT exports rose by more than seven percentage points between 1994 and 2001, it stagnated after that.

On the other hand, and in terms of competitiveness and threat, we find that in all three levels of manufacturing (low-tech, medium-tech, and high-tech manufacturing), Mexico is under direct threat from China for the 2000–2006 period (table 5.3. Again, as discussed in more detail in

TABLE 5.3 DRCP by Technology Level: Mexico vs. China

Tech Level	Mexico		China	
	1995–2000	*2000–06*	*1995–2000*	*2000–06*
PP	−0.4	0.3	−0.1	0.2
RB	−0.1	0.9	1.0	2.8
LT	3.1	−2.4	4.1	14.6
MT	4.0	−0.2	2.3	5.3
HT	4.8	−0.3	3.9	17.4

NOTE: PP = primary product; RB = resource-based; LT = low technology; MT = medium technology; HT = high technology
SOURCE: Authors' calculations based on United Nations Statistics Division (2009).

the previous chapter, most alarming is the direct threat to HT exports. From 2000 to 2006, Mexico's share in HT in the U.S. market decreased by 0.3 percentage points, whereas China's share increased by 17.4.

Summary and Conclusion

Mexico's fears about China's competition clearly have justification. Indeed, our analysis of international competitiveness shows that over half of Mexico's non-oil exports are under partial or direct threat from their Chinese counterparts. This "threat" comprises all but a handful of Mexico's top twenty exports. What's more, recent changes indicate that Mexico's loss of export competitiveness to China is also reaching its more technologically sophisticated exports. Mexico is losing out in sectors abundant in unskilled labor where value-to-transport costs are cheap. It is holding steady, instead, in assembly sectors such as trucks and autos, where transport costs are more significant and NAFTA's rules of origin serve as local content rules mandating that production stay in North America.

How can this deterioration in Mexico's international competitiveness—particularly in relation to China—be explained? First is the relatively lackluster performance of investment in Mexico over the last two decades. Although the macroeconomic reforms launched in the mid-1980s were aimed at positioning the private sector as the pivotal engine of growth of the Mexican economy, private investment has not stepped up to the plate. In fact, since that earlier period, gross fixed capital formation has never reached more than 22 percent of GDP. This is below the 25 percent benchmark identified by UNCTAD as the minimum investment ratio required to sustain the long-term annual rate of economic expansion of 5 percent that Mexico needs to absorb its increasing labor force.

In contrast, China's gross fixed capital formation as a percent of GDP has been over 40 percent for the same period. Mexico's disappointing investment performance can be partly explained by the fact that the reforms were implemented when the Mexican economy was in deep stagnation, with virtually no access to foreign finance. And later, in the mid-1990s, when foreign funds became available, they tended to almost exclusively benefit large, private conglomerates or the few big enterprises remaining within the public sector (Mattar, Moreno-Brid, and Peres 2003).

But the problem has not only originated in the availability of foreign funds. Domestic credit for investment or productive purposes has also been scarce. Private banks have instead preferred to buy government securities or to lend for consumption or housing.[1] This financial constraint for small and medium firms has become even more binding given that, as part of the shift in macroeconomic strategy, development banks were sized down and their capacities to award loans at preferential or subsidized rates was drastically curtailed.

In addition, in Mexico there has been a relation of complementarity among public and private investment and not necessarily of competition. In fact, the decline of public investment brought about an acute deterioration in Mexico's infrastructure—quantity- and quality-wise— that tended to adversely affect the profitability of many private projects and thus to cut down overall investment below its potential.[2] In other words, in a country where public investment encouraged ("crowded in") private investment, the dramatic reduction in public investment has had a multiplying effect. In addition and with some major exceptions—the auto industry and the maquiladoras—foreign direct investment in Mexico, in general, has tended to flow to the service sector and not to manufacturing. If this lack of investment in manufactures persists, we can only expect that the dynamism of its exports will continue to deteriorate (Mattar, Moreno-Brid, and Peres 2003; Gallagher and Zarsky 2007).

The failure of capital formation to grow at a fast pace—after the years of decline during the debt crisis—has deterred the expansion and modernization of Mexico's productive capacity and simultaneously hindered its competitiveness. Using UNIDO's index of structural variation, it has been shown that between the late 1980s and 2003–04, the change in the composition of Mexico's manufactured exports was equivalent to less than 35 percent of their total volume. If maquiladoras are excluded, the proportion is approximately eight points lower, around 28 percent. However, if the same methodology is applied to the composition of *value added* in manufacturing, the change in the composition in Mexican manufactured exports is found to be less than 15 percent (UNIDO 1997). In other words, there is scant evidence of a significant modernization of Mexico's manufacturing industry.

Another element that has tended to undermine Mexico's international competitiveness, relative to China's, is the evolution of the real exchange rates of the Mexican peso and of the Chinese currency vis-à-vis the U.S. dollar. In the nearly two decades that have elapsed from the mid 1980s, when Mexico began its drastic trade-liberalization process, up until 2006, the peso has appreciated 21 percent against the dollar in real terms (calculated in terms of their relative consumer price indices). In stark contrast, the Chinese currency has depreciated. Comparative data shown in figure 6.2 in the next chapter shows that due to the drastic devaluation of the Mexican peso in 1995, the average level of the real exchange rate of the peso against the U.S. dollar in 2004 was similar to its level back in the early 1990s. Such evolution, reinforced by the systematic depreciation of the Chinese currency, has caused a loss of price competitiveness of Mexican goods in the U.S. market vis-à-vis Chinese imports. In the next chapter (figure 6.2) we show the real exchange gap between China and Mexico.

A different but closely related aspect behind the loss of competitiveness has been the deterioration of the relative prices of tradable goods in comparison to those of nontradable ones. There has been a rather systematic increase in the relative prices of services (nontradables) vis-à-vis manufactures. Compared with 1993, in 2003 the prices of services had increased more than 10 percent relative to the prices of manufactures. This change in relative prices has naturally generated incentives for a shift of investment from the tradable to the nontradable sector,

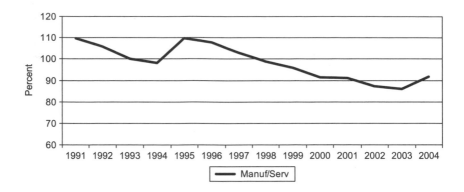

FIGURE 5.1   Mexico: Relative Prices (1993 = 100)
SOURCE: Authors' elaboration based on data from Banco de México (2006); Instituto Nacional de Estadística y Geografía de México (INEGI) (2006).

which makes it all the more difficult to modernize and expand the production of manufactures—indispensable elements to strengthen their international competitiveness.

The laggard performance of total investment has had its toll on the evolution of productivity and unit labor costs. Different estimates indicate that total factor productivity in Mexico has not grown to any significant degree after the macroeconomic reforms. In contrast, China's has increased at a fast pace (Mesquita Moreira 2007). Average real wages, in turn, are certainly higher in Mexico than in China. Such difference tends to more than compensate for the differences in their average levels of productivity that, for the moment, still favor Mexico. Low wages are no longer a comparative advantage of the Mexican economy and, with scant investment, competing in high-tech or more value-added industries will be even harder, if not impossible.

Lastly, Mexico's competitiveness has surely suffered from the shift in the orientation of industrial policies in Mexico away from development programs targeted to promote selected sectors. Up until 1984, Mexican industrial policy was based on strong interventions in specific sectors. Since then, policy in Mexico has been to let markets determine the profile of Mexican manufacturing and exports. As Mesquita Moreira puts it:

> Whether or not these [Chinese] interventionist policies are behind China's takeoff or whether or not they guarantee or compromise China's long

term growth is already the stuff of a prolific policy debate, which, as it happened to other East Asian tigers, is bound to be inconclusive, not least because economists have yet to find a satisfactory way of dealing with the counterfactual. Yet, from LAC manufacturers' point of view, the omnipresence and generosity of the Chinese state has a very practical and immediate implication, that is to heavily tilt the playing field in favor of their Chinese competitors, either local or foreign affiliates, in a scenario where they already face endowment, productivity and scale disadvantages. (Mesquita Moreira 2007)

This substantial difference is so important that the entirety of the next chapter is devoted to a comparative analysis of Chinese and Mexican policies for industrial competitiveness.

6 The State of the State
Industrial Reform in China and Mexico

As we have seen throughout this book, at present the country in LAC most vulnerable to China's expansion is Mexico. Indeed, as we and others have shown, Mexico's competitiveness is sliding downward as China, with its export basket similar to Mexico's, surges ahead. There are other striking similarities between China's and Mexico's economic development over the last quarter century, and there are also significant differences. Thirty years ago, as in Mexico, China's economic model was not performing well, and there was a need for economic reform, including export promotion. Like Mexico, China was a one-party state during the period of reform (although China was and remains "socialist," and Mexico was and remains capitalist, and Mexico democratized in 2000). Like Mexico, China has sought to attract foreign direct investment (FDI) into manufacturing and high-technology sectors to gain access to technology. Both countries have expanded export of manufactured goods, particularly in high- or information-technology industries.

As we will see, this is where the similarities end. China's annual average per capita growth rate has topped 8 percent over this period, whereas Mexico's has been barely over 1 percent. China's annual average growth rate in manufacturing value-added has been well over 10 percent since 1980, whereas Mexico's has been closer to 3 percent. China is becoming the manufacturing powerhouse of the world economy and an increasing source of innovation, moving up the technology ladder from assembly-based manufacturing activity. In Mexico, manufacturing remains at the low end of the technology ladder and is losing its competitiveness relative to China (Dussel Peters 2005, 2007; Gallagher and Porzecanski 2008; Gallagher, Moreno-Brid, and Porzecanski 2008; Pizarro and Shafaeddin 2007).

In this chapter, we show that Mexico's performance is in part a function of a neoliberal mindset that sees a very limited role for the state while integrating into the world economy. China, on the other hand, followed a proactive strategy for its globalization pursuits. Mexico's route to international integration has come at the expense of industrialization and learning; China's proactive approach has made it the manufacturing powerhouse of the world economy.

This chapter is divided into four parts, in addition to the introduction. Following this brief introduction, the first part is a short literature review on industrial learning. Part two examines the case of Mexico, part three analyzes China, and part four summarizes our main findings and draws lessons for research and policy.

The Role of Learning in Industrialization

Regardless of the theoretical framework deployed, the role of learning and capacity-building is seen as paramount for industrial development. Yet, the literature has two poles. On one end, the proponents of governments playing a strong role in industrialization stress "learning-by-doing." By contrast, those in favor of market-led industrialization believe in the contribution of "learning through trading."

Neoclassical or neoliberal approaches to technology and development argue that industrialization comes from "learning through trading." A more heterodox approach argues that industrialization comes about through "learning by doing" and experience. The basic difference between the two is that the first approach does not see a role for government involvement in the learning process, whereas the other, "neodevelopmental" approach argues that governments need to correct market failure and spur technological innovation.

In the neoclassical theory of international trade, technological knowledge and information are freely available—diffusion of knowledge is costless, instantaneous, and automatic. There is no significant learning process, and the development of technology is riskless. All markets are competitive, and comparative advantage is determined by factor cost. As increasing returns and barriers to entry are assumed away, countries that are latecomers to the process of industrialization have no need to invest in human capital and to intervene in the market to promote knowledge-intensive products (which are produced by established firms). Further, there are no static or dynamic externalities. Production costs in different products are not interdependent; there are no spillover effects. Similarly, there are no intertemporal relations between present income/costs and future income/costs, as experience has no place in cost/income determination. In a nutshell, as there is no market or institutional failure, there is no need for any policy intervention.

On the other side, the importance of learning and knowledge accumulation has been emphasized in the postwar and modern theoretical and empirical literature since the publication of the pioneering article on learning by doing by Arrow (1962). To him, the acquisition of knowledge is a product of experience that grows in time. The need for government intervention in learning by doing is articulated in "capability building theory." The theory of capability building (TCB) is built on the infant industry argument of Frederick List, according to which "mental capital," or the accumulation of knowledge and experience, is regarded as the main element of "productive power" [(development) and industrialization. Industrialization in newcomer countries would not take place according to "the natural course of things" (through the operation of market forces alone), and government policies should aim, *inter alia*, at facilitating learning at both the industry and country levels (see Shafaeddin 2005a, 50, for details).[1] The importance of learning and experience in industrialization has also been emphasized by many other scholars (Krugman 1984; Linder 1961; Nelson and Winter 1982).

The theoretical and empirical literature on TCB theory is vast.[2] One strand, the evolutionary theory of TCB, is most relevant for developing countries. The evolutionary version of TCB draws not only on the infant industry argument but also on the evolutionary theory of change (Nelson and Winter 1982) and new growth theory (see Lucas 1988; Romer 1986, 1987). Scholars[3] of this version of TCB regard technological capabilities (learning) and technology absorption and diffusion as the backbone of industrialization and international competitiveness (e.g., Teubal 1987). They define technological capabilities (TCs) in a very broad sense at all levels of activities of firms (i.e., beyond the technique of production) as *"the information and skills—technical, organizational and institutional—that allow productive enterprises to utilize equipment and information efficiently"* throughout the value chain (Lall 1993, 7, italics added). Evolutionary theory also considers the interaction of a firm with other firms and the external environment in obtaining inputs, in the sale and marketing of its products, and particularly in the innovation of new products and processes.

In contrast to neoclassical theory, under TCB, technology is not freely available. The market fails to develop technological capabilities automatically due to reasons of dynamic externalities and linkages, lack of information, uncertainties, risks, and missing and malfunctioning markets. Technological learning involves costs and takes time. It does not take place instantaneously because the required learning is a long, costly, and evolutionary process. It requires purposeful efforts by enterprises as well as government to pursue policies for capability building through research and development (R&D), development of knowledge, and organizational change, particularly at the early stages of industrialization (Moore 1997, 516; Schmitz and Hewitt 1991, 190; Teubal 1996, 449). According to this theory, government policies should be both functional and selective. Selective and targeted intervention, in particular is necessary because learning is technology-specific, firm-specific, and activity-specific, and technologies differ in their tacit features and externalities (Lall 2005). Further, all activities and industries cannot be developed at the same time because of the scarcity of skills and other resources (Shafaeddin 2005b).

R&D for development of domestic technological capabilities and upgrading is the backbone of TCB. R&D is seen as being so important that even some neoclassical economists advocate direct subsidization of knowledge acquisition and R&D (Baldwin 1969). The experience of many developing countries with traditional import substitution indicates that learning from experience alone is not sufficient for building up necessary technological capabilities; appropriate policies are required to overcome market failures constraining development of technological capabilities[4] (Bell, Ross-Larson, and Westphal 1984). In fact, in the case of Asian newly industrializing countries (NICs), government policies and close cooperation between the government and the private sector were crucial in promoting technological capabilities for industrialization and upgrading and for remedying the related obstacles (see, e.g., Lall 2005).

In the age of globalization, government action to enhance firms' capabilities to achieve competitive advantage becomes more important than before because the minimum entry barriers and skill requirements have become higher and risks involved in entry of firms of developing countries into new activities has increased (Archibugi and Michi 1997, 121; Shafaeddin 2005c Lall 2005). However, FDI may provide certain skill and marketing channels for exports. Further, it is argued that when an economy opens up to trade and FDI, an initial period of imitation will lead to a large catch-up opportunity followed by a shift toward innovation "as the knowledge gap is reduced and the economy's technical maturity rises" (Elkan 1996). However, a test of the impact of FDI on the industrialization of a developing country is its affect on development of local capabilities, through spillover channels of demonstration effects, training effects, and linkages effects (Paus 2005). Such capabilities can be influenced by learning, experience, skill development, and the accumulation of knowledge by the labor force of the host country. Generally speaking, the findings of literature on the spillover effects of the FDI on the host country are mixed (for a comprehensive review of this literature, see Görg and Greenaway 2004).

While learning and technological development are firm-specific, they are also activity-specific. For example, "the learning curve differs across quite similar products such as distinct types of memory chips" (Gruber 1992, 885). High-tech industries, which began in Mexico and China at the assembly-operation stage, are both supply-dynamic and demand-dynamic. They are supply-dynamic because they can provide important linkages with other industries and their learning effects in the economy. They are demand-dynamic because international trade in these products has been expanding rapidly during recent decades. Therefore, while looking at the general process of processing industries in Mexico and China, we will, in particular, look into development of these industries.

Our aim in this chapter is to investigate how policies have contributed to the success of China in the accumulation of knowledge necessary for enhancing local value-added in exports, which have been absent in the case of Mexico. Our main focus will be on R&D and its role in the process of industrialization, although some other contributing factors to development of capability of local firms will be discussed as well.

From Learning to Hoping: Mexican Industrial Strategy Under NAFTA

While Mexico's industrial strategy was radically transformed over the past quarter century, the goal has remained the same: "catch-up" with the industrialized world in industrial technologies and capabilities. Up until 1984, the core strategy for meeting these objectives was a government-led model of learning, where Mexico actively pursued the development of technological capabilities through government policy (though not very successfully). Since 1984, however, the core means to industrialization has been market-led. In recent decades government policy has been restricted to creating an environment for foreign investment in the hopes that FDI would bring technological know-how that would automatically spill over into the broader economy.

Over both periods Mexico has certainly aimed at becoming an industrialized country. Mexico has diversified away from an economy primarily based on primary products, has received unprecedented amounts of FDI, and has significantly boosted exports. However, these inroads have come at considerable cost. Mexico has become plagued by a lack of linkages between foreign firms and the domestic economy, painfully low levels of technological capacity building, low valued added in exports of the maquiladora sector, an overdependence on the United States as a chief export market, and a lack of competitiveness vis-à-vis China.

ISI and Industrial Learning

In Mexico and elsewhere, the tools of Import Substituting Industrialization (ISI) focus on a number of key policies, including major public investment in infrastructure; import tariffs, licenses, and quotas to buffer domestic firms and enhance their technological capabilities; exchange rate controls, and direct government investment in key sectors (Fernández 2000). Through this process, Mexico attempted to create "national leaders" in the form of key state-owned enterprises (SOEs) in the petroleum, steel, and other industries. These sectors were linked to chemical, machinery, transport, and textiles industries that also received government patronage (Amsden 2001 Baer 1971). Indeed, in the first decades after World War II, these sectors received over 60 percent of all investment, public and private.

In addition to SOEs and state-patronized private industries, Mexico established export-processing zones called maquiladoras in the mid-1960s. Maquiladoras are "in-bond" assembly factories where imports of unfinished goods enter Mexico duty-free provided that the importer posts a bond guaranteeing the export of the finished good. Many maquiladoras are located in the U.S.-Mexico border region and include industries in electronics and nonelectrical machinery, much of the automotive industry, and apparel. The SOEs, state-patronized private enterprises, and maquiladoras supplied growing internal and external markets with their production.

From the beginning of World War II until the early 1980s, this strategy had mixed results in Mexico. In terms of income growth, this period is often referred to as Mexico's "Golden Age." During this time, the economy grew at an annual rate of over 6 percent, or over 3 percent in per capita terms (Cypher 1990). What's more, public investment appeared to crowd in private investment. According to one study examining the period 1950–1990, for every 10 percent increase in public investment, there was a corresponding bump in gross private capital formation of 2–3 percent (Ramírez 1994).

To some extent, policies geared toward buttressing domestic firms from foreign competition resulted in the learning of complex manufacturing capabilities and the creation of some industries and firms that still exist today. However, the policies were not geared toward the penetration of foreign markets, and therefore the learning that was occurring in the country was not at the technological frontier and could not benefit from a process of learning by competing. Finally, the protective support for industrial learning was not given a well-defined end date and therefore did not provide the incentive for firms to get ready to compete in global markets without support (Fernández 2000).

Market-Led Industrialization

During late 1970s and early 1980s, much of the industrial development strategy was financed through oil revenue (or borrowing against expectations of future oil revenue). As a result, the Mexican government and private sector embarked upon a period of virtually gluttonous borrowing and public spending. The borrowing binge, coupled with a fixed nominal exchange rate, generated a large external debt. The increased borrowing also caused rising inflation, growing real-exchange-rate appreciation, and renewed current-account deficits (Kehoe 1995). From 1970 to the early 1980s, Mexico's foreign debt rose from $3.2 billion to more than $100 billion (Otero 1996). When oil prices suddenly dropped in 1982, a time of high world interest rates, Mexico announced that it was unable to meet its debt obligations—a "watershed event" for most developing countries (Rodrik 1999). A major devaluation plunged Mexico into economic crisis.

In response to the crisis, Mexico abandoned its state-led industrialization strategy to pursue a market-led strategy. Influenced by international institutions and a rising level of domestic constituents frustrated with past policy, in response to this crisis Mexico completely reoriented its development strategy after 1982. The most decisive changes came under President Carlos Salinas de Gortari (1988–1994). Salinas articulated three overarching goals: (1) achieve macroeconomic stability, (2) increase foreign investment, and (3) modernize the economy (Lustig 1998). As in the past, the heart of the plan lay in the manufacturing sector. By opening the economy and reducing the role of the state in economic affairs, Mexico hoped to build a strong and internationally competitive manufacturing sector.

Meeting these goals required a top-to-bottom revamping of Mexico's foreign and domestic economic policies. From 1985 to the present, Mexico has signed over twenty-five trade or investment deals, with NAFTA as the capstone (Wise 1998). To make investments less cumbersome for foreign firms, Mexico also reformed its technology-transfer requirements. During the ISI period, Mexico's Technology Transfer Law was geared toward strengthening the bargaining positions of the recipients of foreign technology. All technology transfers had to be approved by the Ministry of Trade and Industrial Promotion, which monitored the extent to which technology transfer could be assimilated, generated employment, promoted research and development, increased energy efficiency, controlled pollution, and enhanced local spillovers. In 1990, this agency was dismantled with a new technology transfer law, which relinquished all government interference in the technology process to the parties involved in FDI. Government-enforced conditions on technology transfer were phased out, and technology agreements no longer needed government approval (although they had to be registered). Moreover, the law now contains strict confidentiality clauses (UNCTC 1992).

These trade and investment policies set the stage for FDI in the manufacturing sector to be the engine of Mexican development. There were also changes in domestic policies in order to encourage the manufacturing sector to align with the new, neoliberal macroeconomic, trade, and investment policies. In a marked split from the past, Mexico's overarching approach to industrial policy became "horizontal." Rather than targeting a handful of firms and industries as it had done under ISI, the state was to treat all firms and sectors equally, without preference or subsidy. In a horizontal fashion, the state liberalized imports along with exports, phased out subsidies and price controls, and privatized all but a handful of SOEs (Dussel Peters 1999, 2003).

Performance of the New Strategy

The performance of industrial development in Mexico has been uneven, at best. On the positive side, Mexico has diversified away from primary products, upgraded the sophistication of some of its manufacturing export sectors, and increased the level of exports and investment. On the other hand, there has been very little technological learning for the majority of domestic firms, nor has there been linkage between the maquiladora manufacturing enclaves and the rest of the economy. Furthermore, Mexican manufacturing has become dangerously linked to the U.S. economy where—as we conclusively showed in the last chapter— it is losing competitiveness to China.

Indeed, Mexico has transformed itself from a primary products–based economy to one that is more diversified, with a much stronger participation of manufacturing and services. In 1940, agriculture accounted for 22 percent of total output. By the early 1970s, agriculture had shrunk to less than 10 percent and in 2005 was just 4 percent of GDP. In 1940, manufacturing was 17 percent of GDP. It reached a peak of 26 percent in 1987 and fell to 18 percent in 2005. The services industry accounted for 50 percent of GDP in the 1960s and close to 70 percent in 2005 (Reynolds 1970; World Bank 2008).

There has also been significant diversity in manufacturing and industrial upgrading within many sectors. Table 6.1 exhibits the top ten

TABLE 6.1   Mexico's Top 10 Exports to the World

Rank	1980	1990	2005
1	Petroleum	Petroleum	Petroleum
2	Natural gas	Motor vehicles	Motor vehicles
3	Fruit and vegetables	Power generating machinery	Telecommunications equipment
4	Nonferrous metals	Fruit and vegetables	Television receivers
5	Coffee, tea	Nonferrous metals	Motor vehicle parts
6	Fish	Iron and steel	Office machines
7	Motor vehicles	Electrical machinery	Electricity distribution equipment
8	Textile fibers	Organic chemicals	Trucks
9	Inorganic chemicals	Office machines	Electrical machinery
10	Metaliferrous ores	Miscellaneous manufactures	Electrical circuits

SOURCE: Authors' elaboration based on United Nations Statistics Division (2008).

Mexican exports in 1980, 1990, and 2005. Although petroleum is the lead export in each period, the composition of the rest of the top ten is quite different in 2005 than it was in 1980. By 2005, all of the top ten exports (except petroleum), which comprise approximately 75 percent of total exports, are manufactured goods.

The volume of trade and investment has been significant as well. Exports increased by a factor of ten in real terms between 1980 and 2007, and FDI, as a percent of GDP, has increased by a factor of 3 and is close to $20 billion each year (third only to China and Brazil in terms of FDI inflows to developing countries) (UNCTAD 2008; World Bank 2008). The majority of exports and FDI have been in the manufacturing sector, with electronics and the auto sector leading the charge.

Finally, there has been some scattered use of advanced technology and processes within the manufacturing sector, chiefly in the maquiladoras. Researchers drawing on the experiences of Delphi and General Motors depict two other "generations" of maquiladoras in these firms that followed the first generation described above. From 1982 until NAFTA, Multinational Corporations (MNCs) in the maquila industry developed a higher level of technological sophistication and automation, a somewhat more autonomous level of decision-making relative to corporate headquarters, and a relative increase in the number of Mexicans in MNC management tiers. In terms of work organization, the gender mix became a bit more balanced and work was performed in a team atmosphere rather than in traditional assembly production. These firms experienced a "third generation" of innovation in the post-NAFTA period and are characterized by clusters that are formed around technical centers, assembly plants, suppliers of components, and suppliers of services. There was also a greater level of technological development, with an increasing amount of higher-skilled work and engineering capabilities (Carrillo and Hualde 2002).

Despite improvements in diversification, sheer volume of exports, and FDI, such benefits have come at considerable cost. Rather than spurring technological transfer and R&D activities, such transfers have shrunk considerably. FDI has been heavily concentrated by industry and region, is characterized by a growing gap between productivity and wage growth, and has limited linkages with the rest of the Mexican economy (Dussel Peters 2008a; Puyana and Romero 2006; Shafaeddin and Pizarro 2007). In a large study covering fifty-two Mexican industries, Romo Murillo (2002) finds that foreign presence is negatively correlated with backward linkages. Other econometric analyses that looked broadly at the effects of FDI on the Mexican economy between 1970 and 2000 found that investment liberalization was significantly correlated with increases in FDI and subsequent exports, but also led to a higher incidence of imports and the displacement of local firms (Dussel Peters, Lara, and Gomez 2003), and crowding out of domestic investment (Agosin and Machado 2005).

Rather than increasing the amount of R&D, FDI has been negatively correlated with R&D. R&D expenditures by the top twenty foreign firms fell from 0.39 percent of output in 1994 to 0.07 percent in 2002 (Dussel Peters 2008a). Technological decisions for MNCs operating in Mexico are largely made in company headquarters far from Mexico, where technological developments occur and often remain (Unger and Oloriz 2000). A major assessment of FDI and R&D and innovation systems in Mexico concluded that:

> Technological developments occur mainly in the home bases of MNCs and only a small portion is transferred to Mexico. This process ensures, on the one hand, that Mexico participates actively in the globalization of production, and on the other hand, that its participation in the

globalization of scientific and technological activities is very poor. As companies transfer only some of their R&D to Mexico . . . the present concentration of corporate R&D will by and large lead to an even stronger international divergence of technological development. (Cimoli 2000b, 280)

This assessment attributes the poor performance of Mexico's FDI and trade-led learning strategy to a very weak institutional response by Mexico's fledgling innovation system, low levels of interaction between manufacturing sectors and local institutions (finding that public sector or universities were not collaborating with firms), and low levels of technological capacity and coordination among universities.

The assessment characterizes Mexico as having a "maquila innovation system." This is a system that imports technology and equipment and hosts networking activities by MNCs in a manner divorced from the broader economy. The result has been that knowledge and technological advances are kept in developed economies. Imported inputs led to replacement of the learning capabilities that could be built in domestic suppliers of equipment and a virtual wipe-out of many of the firms that had capabilities before reforms. And the personnel working on the limited amounts of R&D are doing so solely within a global MNC network largely divorced from interaction with domestic universities and research centers (Cimoli 2000b).

These findings are depicted in the two graphs in figure 6.1. The top graph exhibits production capacity, competitiveness, and sectoral linkages. During the ISI period there was considerable growth in firms' sectoral domestic linkages and an upward trend in the international competitiveness and production capacities of larger exporting firms. During the transition period out of ISI, the international competitiveness and production capacities of large firms skyrocketed, while the linkages between these exporters and local firms began to diminish in favor of imported inputs. In the post-NAFTA period, the level of competitiveness and capacity reached a plateau (albeit at a high level).

Cimoli's assessment reaches a similar conclusion in terms of technological capabilities, as seen in the second graph. Here, during the ISI period, there was a great deal of domestic firm imitation and innovation of technologies, but these capabilities diminished throughout the reform period as larger foreign export firms (namely maquiladoras) increasingly

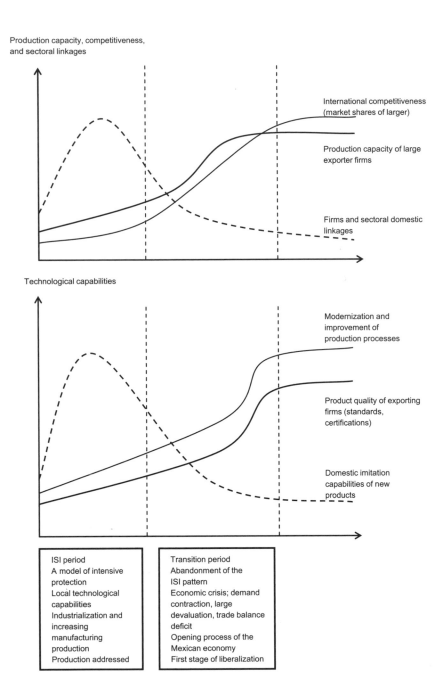

FIGURE 6.1 Mexican Technological Capabilities
SOURCE: Cimoli (2000b, 286).

imported technology. The imported technology did lead to an improvement of production processes and the product quality of exporting firms, which is now at the world technological frontier—albeit due to MNC decisions outside of Mexico.

More recently, the gains in trade and investment flows have become jeopardized. Throughout this transition, Mexico has become increasingly reliant on the U.S. economy. By 2005, 86 percent of all Mexican exports were destined for the United States, and 54 percent of all Mexican imports originated in the United States. Thus, when the U.S. economy slows down, the Mexican economy does so as well. When the United States sneezes, Mexico gets a cold.

Perhaps of greater concern is the fact that Mexico is losing its competitive foothold in the U.S. economy despite its close proximity and favorable tariff access. As we described in previous chapters and in earlier studies (Gallagher, Moreno-Brid, and Porzecanski 2008; Gallagher and Porzecanski 2008), in 2006 more than 80 percent of all Mexican exports to the United States were under some kind of threat, and 97 percent of all of Mexico's high-technology exports to the United States (representing 24 percent of all Mexican exports) were under threat. Indeed, many MNCs are now moving from Mexico to China. A recent study shows that Mexico has now become "proximity dependent." In other words, Mexico is not attracting any new foreign investment in sectors or regions that are not strategic for reexport to the United States (Sargent and Matthews 2008. 2009).

High-Technology Exports

Mexico's FDI-led industrial development strategy is epitomized in the high-technology electronics sector. Built-up during the ISI period, Mexican electronic firms were virtually eliminated after trade liberalization and replaced by a foreign enclave economy with few linkages, minimal R&D, and limited partnerships with universities beyond process innovation. Now, those foreign firms are struggling to compete with China's capabilities, even in the U.S. market.

Mexican endogenous capacities for high-tech manufacturing were seeded and cultivated by ISI policies from the 1940s to the 1980s. Mexico's larger size allowed it to promote the development of the domestic high-tech sector during the ISI period, a sector that became relatively vibrant by the 1980s. Mexico's high-tech antecedents date as far back as the 1940s, when, under ISI protection, national companies began to manufacture radios and radio components. From the 1950s until 1980, Mexican firms manufactured televisions as well as related parts. The government targeted the computer industry in the late 1970s as part of the strategy of the National Council on Science and Technology (CONACYT) to increase Mexico's national self-sufficiency in technology. CONACYT established the PC Program (Programa de Computadoras) to develop a domestic computer industry (supported by the surrounding electronics industry) that would not only serve the domestic market but also emerge as a key exporter for Mexico.

MNCs were limited to 49 percent foreign ownership of firms in the sector. They had to invest between 3 and 6 percent of gross sales into R&D and create research centers and training programs. And domestic parts and components had to account for at least 45 percent of value-added for personal computers and 35 percent for minicomputers. New Mexican-owned firms could receive fiscal credits and low-interest loans from government development banks. In search of domestic markets and export platforms, the foreign firms that came to Mexico were IBM, Hewlett Packard, Digital, NCR, Tandem, and Wang. IBM and Hewlett Packard were the leaders, accounting for 63 percent of all computer production. The other foreign firms were responsible for approximately 18 percent, and wholly owned Mexican firms made up another 18 percent.

The hub of high technology exports became the western state of Jalisco (specifically the Guadalajara city region). Other regions of the country where these firms became concentrated were in the U.S.-Mexico border region (TV monitors) and in the region surrounding Mexico City (electronic appliances). Guadalajara was the ideal region for high-tech FDI, as it had lower wages and weak unions, relative proximity to the United States, low tariffs, and five major universities and numerous technical schools and industrial parks with the capability to host research activity and graduate an adequately skilled workforce (Gallagher and Zarsky 2007).

Furthermore, the government adopted a number of policies to attract MNCs to Mexico. At the national level, one program (called

PITEX) allows firms to import their inputs duty-free as long as more than 65 percent of their output is exported (Dussel Peters 2003). The Jalisco state government supplemented these federal programs with a regional plan to attract firms and suppliers. The state's Economic Promotion Law reduced or eliminated state and municipal taxes for firms that located to the region. In addition, the Guadalajara branch of the national chamber of commerce for the high-tech industry, CANIETI (Cámara Nacional de la Industria, Electrónica, de Telecomunicaciones e Informática) works to attract large MNCs to the region and puts on numerous trade shows and workshops on the industry. A more regional organization named CADELEC (Cadena Productiva de la Electronica) was founded in 1998 with funding from CANIETI, the United Nations Development Program, and two other federal agencies. CADELEC's mission is to match domestic suppliers with the large MNCs (CADELEC 2004; Palacios 2001).

The laissez-faire strategy was a success—at least in terms of attracting investment and increasing exports. Between 1994 and 2000, foreign direct investment in the electronics sector grew by five times and the value of exports quadrupled. At their peaks, exports from Mexico's electronics sector totaled $46 billion in 2000, and FDI inflows totaled $1.5 billion in 1999.

By 2000, high tech was a key component of the Mexican manufacturing economy, accounting for nearly 6 percent of manufacturing output, 27 percent of all exports, 9 percent of employment, and 10 percent of FDI. Electronics are Mexico's largest manufactured export and are second only to autos in terms of manufacturing GDP and employment (Dussel Peters, Lara, and Gomez 2003).

Fueled by large FDI inflows, Mexico's high-tech industry became increasingly competitive during the second half of the 1990s. Mexico's share of world high-tech exports ballooned from 0.8 percent in 1985 to 3 percent in 2000 (Dussel Peters, Lara, and Gomez 2003). By 2001, Mexico was the eleventh largest exporter of high-tech products in the world economy. However, as shown in Chapter 4, Mexico's competitiveness and concentration in high-tech exports (measured as the share of manufacturing exports that are high-tech exports) began to flatten and then decline, particularly when compared to China's.

Evolution of Domestic Firms

Unlike the experience of China, as we will see briefly, in Mexico rapid MNC-led growth came at the expense of the country's domestic high-tech firms, which were virtually wiped out. The domestic high-tech industry is nearly extinct, and few domestic input producers have become integrated into the global production chains of the high-tech MNCs operating in Mexico. Between 1985 and 1997, the number of indigenous electronics firms in Guadalajara declined by 71 percent (Rivera Vargas 2002), and thirteen of the twenty-five indigenous electronics firms that were still in existence at the end of 1997 had been closed by 2005 (Gallagher and Zarsky 2007; Sargent and Matthews 2008, 2009). Indeed, as early as 1998, signs of this decline were already evident when the Economic Commission for Latin America and the Caribbean (ECLAC) concluded that industrialization in the electronics industry had become almost completely "internationalized" and was beginning to resemble a "parallel economy" that had very few linkages in Mexico (ECLAC 1999). Since then, the literature has been quite extensive and too large to cover in this chapter, but key contributions include two edited books by Enrique Dussel Peters (2003, 2004), and a volume by Rivera Vargas (2002).

The linkages between foreign hightech firms and national firms are even more dismal than the national average. Most of the MNCs in the high-tech sector are working with local firms that supply cardboard boxes, shipping labels, cables, wires, and disposal services. This finding suggests that although the share of national inputs has increased, at less than 2 percent of all inputs it still remains very small, and the composition of those inputs has changed from national high-tech firms to national shipping and disposal firms (Gallagher and Zarsky 2007).

Table 6.2 compares Mexico and China in world high-technology markets. In 2000, the year before China entered the WTO, Mexico and China enjoyed global market penetration in computers, peripherals, and telecommunications at similar orders of magnitude. In just five years, China captured 15–29 percent of global high-tech markets, whereas Mexico lost competiveness in each case (Gallagher and Zarsky 2007).

In response to competitive pressure, MNCs in Mexico have been upgrading their product mix. For the most part, they have been able to redirect their generic manufacturing capacities to other products and

TABLE 6.2 China vs. Mexico in World High-Tech Markets

	Computers	Peripherals	Telecom
	(Country exports as a percent of world exports)		
China			
2000 market share	6.0	4.0	5.6
2006 market share	31.5	16.4	2.05
Percentage point change	25.5	12.4	14.8
Mexico			
2000 market share	4.5	2.2	5.2
2006 market share	3.2	1.3	3.2
Percentage point change	−1.2	−0.9	−1.9

SOURCE: Authors' elaboration based on United Nations Statistics Division (2008).

clients. Jabil Circuit, for instance, shifted production to communications switches, specialized hand-held credit card processing machines, Internet firewalls, and electronic controls for washing machines. Solectron is assembling components for mainframes and AX-400 conductivity transmitters. SCI-Sanmina now assembles MRI scanners for Phillips and electronics auto components for Ford and GM. Not all of the MNCs were able to upgrade with this agility, and even in such a ramp-up, national firms continued to be out in the cold. Indeed, most of the contract equipment manufacturers (CMs) have resorted to Internet-based open-supplier bidding, and the winners are other foreign firms (Gallagher and Zarsky 2007; Sargent and Matthews 2008, 2009). In addition, Mexico is also losing ground to China in "non-proximity [to the U.S. market] dependent, technology intensive EPZ manufactures" (Sargent and Matthews 2008).

In short, during in the 1990s Mexico was a poster child for neoliberalism, throwing open its borders to trade and foreign investment, embracing NAFTA, and ending the government's role in fostering industrial learning. The evidence shows that although Mexico was initially successful in attracting multinational corporations, foreign investments waned in the absence of active government support and as China became increasingly competitive. Moreover, the FDI-led innovation and growth strategy created an "enclave economy," the benefits of which were confined to an international sector and not connected to the wider Mexican economy.

In fact, MNCs put many domestic firms out of business and transferred only limited amounts of technology.

The prevailing consensus that Mexico's development model has not performed well should not, however, be interpreted as an argument for returning to the ISI policies of the past. As shown in Figure 6.1, even during the ISI period, Mexico's level of competitiveness, product sophistication, and production capacities was relatively weak. By the end of the ISI period, even the domestic imitation capabilities and the domestic linkages started to cascade as well. Indeed, it is clear that the goal of integrating with the world economy was a good one. The problem was that the pendulum swung too far back, and Mexico's hands-off approach centered on the belief the market would automatically allocate such capabilities. As we will now see, China has similar goals but has followed and continues to follow a different path to achieve them.

Crossing the River by Touching Each Stone: Technological Learning in China

Like Mexico, China embarked on a process of economic reform over a quarter of a century ago. Like Mexico, it has sought to attract FDI into manufacturing and high-technology sectors in order to gain access to technology and marketing channels for exports. Nevertheless, China's industrial development has been very different from Mexico's in two important ways. First, in contrast to Mexico's rapid opening of markets and integration into the world economy, China has taken a more gradual and experimental approach to integration, upgrading, and industrial development. Secondly, alongside reforms, China continued a parallel set of targeted government policies to support and nurture industrial development. Its nurturing of industrial development has been geared toward learning through R&D and aiding domestic firms to develop the capabilities to increase value-added in exports.

From Mao to the Market: Economic Reform in Context

In a somewhat similar fashion to Mexico, China underwent a period of state-led industrialization from the late 1940s until 1978. This period has been referred to as the time of "Big Push Industrialization."

As in Mexico, during the Big Push the government's goal was to move toward rapid industrialization through import substitution. The basic plan was to invest in the strategic industries identified by government decision-makers. The industries selected included those with the largest potential for backward linkages. Integration with the global economy was extraordinarily low (Naugthon 2007).

Eighty percent of the targeted industries were "heavy" industries, such as steel, which were linked with coal, iron ore, machinery and other sectors. A number of other industries such as chemical fertilizers, motor vehicles, and electric generating equipment were also among those created by the government. Almost all of these industries became dominated by state-owned enterprises, and the planners assigned them production targets and prices. The government was also in charge of allocating labor resources to industrial firms. Through one lens this effort was successful, as the industrial base of the country was created. From 1952 to 1978, industrial output grew at an annual rate of 11.5 percent, and the share of industrial sector in GDP increased from 14 to 44 percent, while the share of agriculture fell from 51 to 28 percent (Naugthon 2007).

However, these policies also involved some shortcomings. First and foremost, the focus on industrialization neglected the growth of household consumption and the development of the countryside. Whereas capital formation grew at more than 10 percent per year from 1952 to 1978, private consumption grew only 4.3 annually. Employment generation was also low, given the capital-intensive nature of the main targeted industries. Perhaps the gravest shortcoming was the lack development of technological capabilities by the targeted firms. Further, human capital formation did not expand enough for these sectors to become efficient and competitive internationally (Naugthon 2007).

Chinese economic reforms started in 1978, two years after the death of Mao Zedong. In this year, China embarked on a program of economic reform aiming at strategic integration into the world economy by following a "dual track" policy. The policy consisted of liberalizing FDI and inflow of imported inputs to selected industries while buttressing those sectors to the point of maturity and nurturing other sectors until they were ready to face competition with imports. Since then, according to the literature, China's industrial strategy has been three-pronged.

First, government policy aimed at creating endogenous productive capacity, in the form of targeting specific industries through state ownership or government support, paying increasing attention to science and technology policy, and linking the SOEs with the private sector and research institutes.

Second, and very importantly, Chinese support for domestic industry has always had an eye on markets outside of China. China has also gradually and strategically integrated into world markets in order to gain access to technology and finance and to gradually expose its new industries to world markets.

Third, in undertaking economic reform, China's new leaders followed an experimental approach. Unlike Mexico, China had a much more experimental (trial and error) and less certain attitude toward reform. The Mexican government was ideologically committed to reforming toward a market economy and free trade. In a sense, free trade and a market-based economy were seen as an end in itself in the case of Mexico; it was taken for granted that such a transition by itself would enhance learning through trade and lead to the deepening of industrialization and promotion of growth. By contrast, Chinese policy was based on using the market and trade as a means to development. Hence, in the eyes of Chinese policymakers, market and government policies were to supplement each other while the weight of each would change as the economy developed.

> It was never conceivable to Chinese policy-makers that their economy would postpone economic development until after an interlude of system transformation. It was always assumed that system transformation would have to take place concurrently with economic development, and indeed that the process of economic development would drive market transition forward and guarantee its eventual success. Individual reform policies were frequently judged on the basis of their contribution to economic growth (rather than to transition as such). In the beginning the approach was followed because reformers literally did not know where they were going: they were reforming "without a blueprint" and merely seeking ways to ameliorate the obvious serious problems of the planned economy. But even after the goal of a market economy gradually gained ascendance in the minds of reformers, it was not anticipated that market transition would be completed until the economy reached at least middle-income status. And in fact, that is exactly what eventually happened. (Naugthon 2007, 86)

These policies, discussed in detail below, were enveloped and supported for a long time by an undervalued exchange rate. This made China's export goods much cheaper in world markets, especially relative to Mexico's. Figure 6.2 exhibits the real exchange rate (local currency to the USD) in China and Mexico from 1985 to 2008. In the case of Mexico it is clear that the Chinese yuan is depreciating in real terms relative to the U.S. dollar and the Mexican peso is appreciating. As we discussed in Chapter 5, while China deliberately manipulated its currency to overvalue it, Mexico's tight fiscal policies made its exchange rate persistently overvalued.

Many attribute China's rise to its very low wages relative to those in Mexico and others in LAC. In terms of wages in manufacturing as a whole, China's wages are four (Brazil) to seven (Mexico) times lower than their LAC counterparts (Mesquita Moreira 2007). In terms of productivity, however, the story is much more nuanced. Mesquita Moreira of the Inter-American Development Bank finds that productivity is fairly even between China and Mexico for consumer electronics, and that Brazil's is

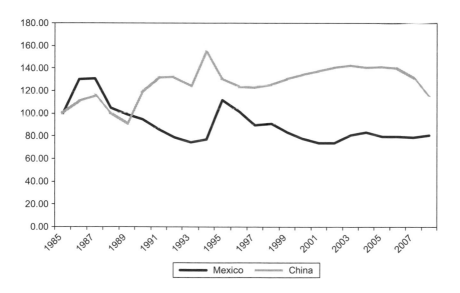

FIGURE 6.2 Chinese and Mexican Real Exchange Rates in Comparative Perspective (local currency to the USD)
SOURCE: Author's elaboration with data from USDA Economic Research Service (2009).

higher. For personal computers, China lags behind both Brazil and Mexico. However, productivity growth (rather than productivity levels) in the three countries tells a radically different story, according to Mesquita Moreira. Since 1990 productivity in manufacturing as a whole in Brazil and Mexico has grown by a factor of approximately 1.4, but manufacturing productivity in China has leaped by a factor of almost 7.

China's gradual and experimental approach to reform allowed for the development of domestic firms and industries before liberalization was fully implemented. More importantly, it also created an environment so that the potential "losers" from liberalization would be less numerous (Naugthon 2007). Components of market and planned economies coexisted in this dual-track policy, which has been referred to as a "socialist market economy" in the literature (see, for example, Singh 1993).

The Role of R&D

Unlike in Mexico, where it was assumed that technology would be transferred through trade and FDI, conscious attention to science and technology (S&T) policy and research and development (R&D) has been a cornerstone of China's policy for industrial development and integration into the world economy. The Chinese government learned in practice that technology acquisition from abroad through MNCs alone would not necessarily lead to the transfer and development of technology; there was a need to increase the absorptive capacity of domestic firms and the development of indigenous technological capacity building. To accomplish this, the strategy of the Chinese government included government support, indigenous R&D and innovation investment within individual firms, and creation of R&D institutions. It also included alliance among firms in an industry and their cooperation with research institutes and universities, as well as foreign firms, targeting in particular the industries considered to be strategic for industrialization (Qian 2003).

Government policy ranged from direct investment to provision of guidance, institutional and financial support, and creating a favorable environment for innovation, as well as the introduction of competition into the domestic market for the strategic industries (e.g., telecommunication) (Fan, Gao, and Watanabe 2007, 359) and the development of national standards and patents for main high-tech products (Wang and

Wang 2007). The science and technology (S&T) strategy of the government also aimed at a long-term goal of upgrading the industrial base of the country. It was selective, targeted, and responsive to market dynamics, with growing emphasis on the private sector (including MNCs). Beginning in the early 1980s, China put in place a number of policies that not only aimed at conducting basic research but also put equal emphasis on the deployment and diffusion of technology. Table 6.3 provides a snapshot of China's key S&T policies between 1982 and 2000.

TABLE 6.3 Development of China's National Innovation System

Policy	Dominant Feature	Year
Key technology R&D program	Encouraging efforts in key technologies	1982
Resolution on the reform of S&T system (CCCP)	Adopting flexible system on R&D management	1985
Sparkle system 5	Promoting basic research in agriculture 1	1985
863 program	High-tech promotion	1986
Torch program	High-tech commercialization, high-tech zones	1988
National S&T achievements spreading program	Promoting product commercialization	1990
National Engineering Technology Research Center program	Technology transfer and commercialization of research	1991
Climbing program	Promoting basic research	1992
Endorsement of UAEs by SSTCC	Promoting university and industry linkage	1992
S&T progress law	Technology transfer, S&T system reform	1993
Decision accelerating S&T progress (CCCP)	Promoting URI-industry linkage	1995
Law for promoting commercialization of S&T achievement	Regulating the commercialization of S&T achievement	1996
Super 863 program	Commercialization, breakthrough in key areas	1996
Decision on developing high-tech industrialization	Encouraging technology innovation and commercialization	1999
Guidelines for developing national university science parks	Accelerating the development of university science parks	2000

SOURCE: Xiwei and Xiangdong (2007).

The government apparatus for guiding the S&T consisted of six different entities: the Chinese Academy of Science together with five relevant ministries, including the Ministry of Information Technology, which was specifically created for supporting high-tech industries (Xiwei and Xiangdong 2007, 318). The national system of innovation was geared to basic research as well as R&D in selective activities. The 863 Program (1986) aimed at high basic and applied research in seven areas and fifteen topics with the cooperation of private enterprises. The seven areas included, in order of priority given by the planners, information technology, laser, automation, biotechnology, new material technology, astrotechnology, and energy technology (Fan and Watanabe 2006, 311). The "climbing program" of 1992 was oriented toward acceleration of basic research. By contrast, from inception in 1988, the Torch program was market-oriented and geared mainly toward the commercialization of R&D results. Its objectives ranged from enabling an environment for high-tech industries to creation of high-tech zones, executing projects in the aforementioned selected seven areas, and training and facilitating international cooperation (Fan and Watanabe 2006, 312). In 1995 the government passed the "Decision on Accelerating Scientific and Technological Progress" in order to intensify the technological development (Walsh 2003, 105).

The ninth five-year plan (1996–2000) specifically emphasized the development of capabilities to increase domestic value-added in assembly operations in the computer industry and its peripherals. This was followed by the emphasis on innovation in integrated circuits and software technology in the tenth five-year plan (2001–5) under the so-called "Golden Projects" (Xiwei and Xiangdong 2007, 321).

The national system of innovation (NIS) was dynamic in terms of both institutional development and the change in the relative role of government and private enterprises. The S&T system of China consisted of universities, research institutes, and public and private enterprises, including foreign firms. The interrelationship between universities/research institutes and industry is regarded as unique (Chen and Kenney 2008). Furthermore, the system went through continuous reforms in terms of policies and the involvement of actors in R&D. To benefit from "collective efficiency" through clustering, a number of high-tech zones (technology parks) were established (by 1992, fifty-two high-tech zones had been established) (Xiwei and Xiangdong 2007, 319).[5]

Close links were also developed among enterprises, universities, and research institutes. Further, commercialization of R&D was encouraged in China. In particular, over time, the role of private enterprises in R&D increased significantly. Between 1987 and 2003 the number of R&D institutes increased by 67 percent. By 2003, however, the number of public institutes decreased while the institutes led by the private sector (enterprise) more than doubled. This trend is mimicked in terms of spending. In 1987, 60.7 percent of R&D expenditure was undertaken by public institutes. By 2003, the share of the private sector in China was 62.4 percent and that of research institutes and universities was 36 percent (Table 6.5). The distinction between private and public entities involved in R&D is blurred, however, as some universities and research institutes own enterprises engaged in research (Chen and Kenney 2008).

Expenditure and policy have not been horizontal, but have been targeted to the specific sectors and industries as outlined above. In allocating R&D expenditures, China has targeted a handful of sectors, namely the electronics, semiconductor, and automotive industries, to eventually serve as "national champions" (Xiwei and Xiangdong 2007).

The comparison of China and Mexico is striking in terms of both input to and the results of the S&T policies. China's expenditure on R&D (as a percentage of GDP and in per capita terms) far exceeds that of Mexico in both level and change over time. In fact, the difference in the performance of the two countries becomes more revealing when one compares the growth rates of expenditures in relative terms. Over 1996–2004, Mexico's expenditure (in USD and PPP) merely doubled, while China's increased by a factor of 5. China's indicators for R&D are the highest in Asia after Singapore, South Korea, and Taiwan; they are also higher than those of Spain and Italy. In 2004, the number of people working on R&D in China was over 1.15 million, or 13.4 per 1,000 of population, as compared with the 60,039 people (0.59 per 1.000 of population) working on R&D in Mexico in 2003 (UNCTAD 2009. In 2003, China had 17.1 research institutes per million people.

Another difference between the two countries is the change in the role that private enterprises played in R&D. The relatively hands-off approach deployed by the Mexican government on the activities of private firms did not motivate them to increase their involvement in R&D as was the case in China, where the government provided guidance and support.

According to data provided by UNESCO, the share of business enterprises in gross domestic expenditure on R&D in Mexico increased from 22.4 percent in 1996 to 31.7 percent in 2004. By contrast, the corresponding figures for China were an increase from 43.3 percent to 68.3 percent (Xiwei and Xiangdong 2007). Similarly, business enterprises' contribution to the sources of R&D funding in China increased from 18 percent in 1985 to 32.4 percent in 1994 and 60.2 percent in 2003 (Xiwei and Xiangdong 2007). In other words, unlike the case of Mexico, private enterprises have become the driving force in R&D activities where seven firms were main actors involved in targeted technology areas.[6]

The results of the implementation of S&T policy are striking for China when compared with Mexico's experience. On average, more patents are filed in China each year than in all of the Latin American countries combined, let alone Mexico. Furthermore, whereas in LAC only 13 percent of all patents are held by residents, in China that figure is above 75 percent. Similar results are also evident when comparing the number of articles published by Chinese scholars with the number published by Latin American scholars. Moreover, the relative importance of inventions has increased sharply over time (Table 6.4). It is true that the share of domestic firms in total patents and in patents granted for invention has decreased since the accession to WTO in 2000 (table 6.4) because of the increasing involvement of foreign companies in China. Nevertheless, the absolute number of invention patents granted to domestic firms accelerated sharply during the period from 2000 to 2005. The annual average growth rate of invention patents granted to domestic firms was 27.3 percent during 2005 as compared with 18.3 percent during 1990–2000.

Training

In tandem with R&D, China has a high level of support for tertiary education and training. Over 20,000 scientists and engineers graduate from Chinese universities each year (MOST 2006). The high level of education in science and technology, as well as the existence of facilities

TABLE 6.4 Selected Science and Technology Indicators

	1980–2005	*2000–2005*
East Asia and Pacific		
Patent applications, nonresidents	27,119	64,235
Patent applications, residents	17,387	44,106
Patent applicatiions, resident share	**64.12%**	**68.66%**
Research and development expenditure (% of GDP)	0.89	1.09
Scientific and technical journal articles	11,505	24,804
China		
Patent applications, nonresidents	24,236	58,876
Patent applications, residents	18,785	43,509
Patent applicatiions, resident share	**77.51%**	**73.90%**
Research and development expenditure (% of GDP)	0.98	1.21
Scientific and technical journal articles	10,386	22,979
Latin America and the Caribbean		
Patent applications, nonresidents	19,044	29,850
Patent applications, residents	3,792	4,056
Patent applicatiions, resident share	**19.91%**	**13.59%**
Research and development expenditure (% of GDP)	0.57	0.57
Scientific and technical journal articles	9,666	16,472
Mexico		
Patent applications, nonresidents	7,051	12,745
Patent applications, residents	540	498
Patent applicatiions, resident share	**7.65%**	**3.91%**
Research and development expenditure (% of GDP)	0.39	0.41
Scientific and technical journal articles	2,026	3,488

SOURCE: World Bank (2008).

for vocational education, facilitates the training of skilled manpower for technological development. In 2005, the number of graduates in the fields of science and technology from universities and junior colleges was 1,256,000 or over 1,000 per million people. In the same year the corresponding number of graduates from postgraduate courses was 95000, or over 90 per million.[7] Continuous attention to education was a characteristic of the overall Chinese development strategy before, as well as after, the reform period. According to the World Bank, government expenditure on tertiary education per student was 90 percent of GDP per capita in 1999 (in Mexico that figure was 48 percent for the same year) (World Bank 2008).

Comprehensive information on the training program of the government is lacking. Nevertheless, there are indications that the government focused on enhancing high-tech skills and education by establishing state funding training centers (Walsh 2003, 71). Some universities were also involved in training, with a number of them benefiting from partnership with MNCs for training in addition to R&D (Walsh 2003, 83). The Beijing University of Post and Communication is one example of cooperation with MNCs in training. Foreign investors also independently provided some training of local staff (Walsh 2003, 96).

The government created a large number of vocational schools. In 2005, there were 198,566 vocational schools in China, of which 11,611 were secondary schools and 4,230 were technical training. The number of graduates for vocational secondary schools increased by over twenty-one times between 1978 and 2005 (People's Republic of China 2006, table 2-10). Further, the government policy of sending students abroad helped the development of domestic skills in research and development even though some of them never returned to China. The combination of these factors allowed the rapid expansion of persons engaged in scientific and technical activities in more recent years, resulting in an increase by over 21 percent during 2001–5 when 3,810,000 were engaged in this area (People's Republic of China 2006, table 21-36). There remains, however, a lack of upper management staff despite the fact that some Chinese who have studied and worked abroad have returned to the country.

Other Measures to Build Up Capabilities of National Enterprises

In contrast to Mexico, the main motive behind the development of capabilities of domestic firms was the realization by the government and national enterprises that the transfer of technology from MNCs did not occur automatically (Fan, Gao, and Watanabe 2007, 360). Under joint ventures there was a limit to the transfer of technology to Chinese partners (Walsh 2003, 113). The effort to develop capabilities of domestic firms, in turn, simulated the rivalry among MNCs to be involved in

R&D programs of domestic firms in order to not be denied access to the large Chinese market.

The Chinese government has followed a gradual and dual policy in developing the capabilities of domestic enterprises. It has gradually increased the role of private firms in the process of industrialization and export expansion. For example, the share of private enterprises in exports has increased from 18 percent in 1985 to 60 percent in 2005 (Naugthon 2007). At the same time, it has, implicitly or explicitly, established a division of labor between SOEs and private enterprises. The private enterprises have emphasized, as expected, short-term opportunities and low-cost production and sale to achieve high profitability. By contrast, SOEs concentrated on long-term goals through investment for development of new products rather than profitability per se (Li and Xia 2008). In their efforts, SOEs benefited little from spillover effects from MNCs (Girma and Gong 2008). SOEs were privileged to have better access to government funds and loans from the banking system (Li and Xia 2008).

In their applied R&D, SOEs benefited from a program called National Science and Technology Diffusion, which was specifically designed for and devoted to them. This strategy is criticized for not having market-oriented goals in the case of SOEs. This lack is important, particularly because SOEs had had social objectives and responsibilities in addition to their long-term technological goals.

To provide sources of investment for domestic firms, China established two funds: the Export Development Fund for the larger firms and the Fund for Small and Medium Enterprise Incursions into International Markets for suppliers. The government also offered value-added tax refunds to exporting firms, and the Chinese Export-Import Bank provided loans with preferential interest rates.

Chinese domestic firms enjoyed the advantage of familiarity with the domestic market, as well as being allocated a significant part of the domestic market by the government (e.g., in the telecom equipment industries) (Fan, Gao, and Watanabe 2007, 358). Still, the newcomer domestic firms in China, like enterprises in other developing countries, suffered from two main disadvantages as compared with MNCs in the development of capabilities for and commercialization of new technology. They faced resource disadvantages and reputation disadvantages, particularly in the high-tech sector where the technology is complicated and changes rapidly (Gao et al. 2007). Provided with incentives as well as support by the government together with some capabilities developed during the import substitution period, however, a number of firms have managed to break into the market by developing frontier technologies (see below). In addition to the support from the government, the leading domestic firms collaborate with customers and cooperate with MNCs (Gao et al. 2007).

The Role of FDI

The contribution of MNCs to the financial resources needed for R&D has been small. Nevertheless, they have become increasingly involved in R&D in China. Foreign high-tech R&D in China has gone through three phases: explanatory and strategic partnership (early to mid-990s), expansion (mid- to late 1990s) and consolidation (late 1990s to present) (Walsh 2003, 86–91). During the 1990s, foreign investment in R&D was more of a "show" than a genuine action, such as establishing meaningful R&D facilities. This was the case because R&D was a precondition for obtaining approval to establish joint ventures. During the second phase, the MNCs also started to expand training centers. It was during the third phase that the MNCs became interested in moving up the value-added production chain to upgrade their products and thus needed to invest in local R&D (Walsh 2003, 86–91).

Meanwhile, the Chinese government also provided "a range of preferential policies, including tax rebates, construction loans, access to modern facilities and other incentives" for the MNCs, particularly in the case of high-tech industries (Walsh 2003, xiii and 56). While encouraging foreign firms to undertake R&D in China, the authorities initially entered into partnerships with a number of foreign firms to create interfirm rivalry and to accelerate technological development (Walsh 2003, 77–78 and 80–82). As a result, wholly foreign-owned firms established R&D facilities in the country (Walsh 2003, 79). Attracting multiple foreign partners was particularly successful in the information technology (IT) industry. It is estimated that around 120 to 400 foreign R&D centers were operational in 2003 (Walsh 2003, xiv). In the case of IT industries, since early 1990s, almost all main MNCs involved have established R&D centers in China. In Beijing alone, 18 main centers were established between 1993 and 2003.[8] Domestic firms also benefited, to some extent, from the partnership with MNCs. For example, Legend, Stone, Founder and Great Wall learned a great deal about modern manufacturing in addition to technology development (Walsh 2003, 79). Nevertheless, the Chinese authorities realized that joint ventures with MNCs alone would not be sufficient for technology transfer.

Generally speaking, in China, unlike Mexico, FDI has crowded in domestic investment as government efforts aimed at building capabilities of domestic firms. As predicted by TCB, such capabilities in turn motivated MNCs to invest in R&D. As domestic firms were involved in development of their technological capabilities, many MNCs were motivated to join them in their R&D in order to access the domestic market, particularly since—as described above—the government also provided them with other incentives.

In China, efforts to indigenously develop technological capabilities and to bring such technologies to market have been coupled with a targeted but aggressive acquisition of foreign technologies through foreign direct investment. The strategy has been either to develop a sector or technology nationally or to "import" the technology through FDI. Initially, licensing FDI was conditioned on arrangements for transfer of technology and provision of linkages to local firms, joint ventures, and partnership. In 2001, such conditions were dropped. However, the government still encourages MNCs to invest in R&D, particularly in information technology, "by offering a range of preferential policies that includes tax rebates, construction loans, access to modern facilities, and other incentives" (Walsh 2003, xiii and 56). Whereas national Mexican firms capture only approximately 5 percent of the inputs of foreign firms, in China that number is well over 20 percent (Gallagher and Zarsky 2007).

High-Tech Industries

China is the most impressive contemporary case of latecomer high technology development.[9] For twenty-five years, the country gradually and quietly built manufacturing capacities and integrated into world markets. China has been at the core of MNC location strategies because of its multiple location-specific assets: a large and growing internal market *and* a low-cost export platform for manufactured goods. Furthermore, China provides a match for national linkage capability between MNCs and domestic suppliers. Now the country is on the verge of having formidable flagship firms of its own in the high-tech industry.

High-tech FDI in China has gone through four phases: sale, marketing, licensing, and technical services; manufacturing and production; product design, localization and redevelopment; and finally R&D (Walsh 2003, 75–76). Much is made of China's low wages as a major factor driving MNC outsourcing to China and high-tech development more generally. There is little doubt that wages are low: the average manufacturing wage in China was estimated to be 61 cents an hour in 2001, compared to $16.14 in the United States and $2.08 in Mexico (Federal Reserve Bank of Dallas 2003). But the story of China's success and likely emergence as the center for global high-tech production goes beyond low wages and generic product manufacturing capabilities. As we saw in Chapter 5, wages are part but not all of the story.

The development of the high-tech industry in China is the result of a combination of government intervention, foreign investment, and entrepreneurship. In 1986, four Chinese scientists recommended to the government that high tech be designated as a strategic sector. The request was approved, and in 1988, China's National Development and Reform Commission (formerly the State Planning Commission) designated high tech as a "pillar" industry worthy of strategic industrial policy (MOST 2006). It was coupled with MOST's National High Tech R&D (or 863) Program that supported R&D efforts of local governments, national firms, and regions. The goal was to foster a vibrant high-tech sector with national firms that could eventually compete as global flagships. The strategy was to establish domestic firms and bring foreign firms to China in order to build their capacity to produce components and peripherals for PCs. To this end, IBM, HP, Toshiba, and Compaq were all invited to come to China and form joint ventures with such Chinese firms as Legend, Great Wall, Trontru, and Star. As mentioned above, China required the foreign firms to transfer specific technologies to the joint venture, establish R&D centers, source to local firms, and train Chinese employees

(USDOC 2006). By the 1990s, all of the major contract equipment manufacturers also had formed joint ventures with Chinese firms under similar arrangements. According to the tenth five-year plan, ending in 2005, the government planned to invest more than $120 billion in the high-tech industries in order to raise the share of the sector to 7 percent of GDP (Walsh 2003, 71)

The strategy has paid off. "By carefully nurturing its domestic computing industry through tightly controlled partnerships with foreign manufacturers," concludes Dedrick, "China has become the fourth-largest computer maker in the world" (Dedrick and Kraemer 2002: 28). Indeed, the majority of foreign electronics firms in China are either joint ventures or domestic/state-owned enterprises (SOEs). In the personal computer industry for instance, Hewlett Packard and Dell do have stand-alone operations in China, though China's Lenovo, Founder, and Tong fang do as well. However, many more are joint ventures such as IBM-Great Wall, Toshiba-Toshiba Shanghai, Epson-Start, and Taiwan GVC and TCL (Rodrik 2006).

Given the large nature of the economy and the fact that China serves as an export platform, China has had a great deal of bargaining power vis-à-vis MNCs. First, China had location-specific assets that could not be ignored. Not only did China offer an export platform like those of Taiwan and South Korea, it also had a large and growing domestic market, which is a major bargaining chip for any country trying to lure FDI. In essence, foreign firms traded market access for technology transfer. In this respect, China's experience may well be unique and not replicable around the world. China's domestic market continues to grow rapidly, propelled not only by a rise in personal income but also by the active government promotion strategies previously mentioned.

In addition to domestic market access, global MNCs have been willing to work in the confines of Chinese policy because of China's active support for and subsidies to the high-tech industry. According to a comprehensive study by Dussel Peters (2005), a key program has been the establishment of high-tech industrial parks. Much of the FDI flows to these parks, where it is matched with national firms that are the recipients of numerous incentives and assistance programs. Despite the potential market payoffs, foreign firms are now starting to get nervous about technology transfer arrangements, especially as Chinese high-tech firms begin to emerge as flagship companies. Indeed, OECD governments have begun to dub China's policies "forced transfers" and have undertaken investigations and task forces in order to eliminate or reduce them (USDOC 2006).

Another key element of the strategy is a high level of support for high-tech R&D and education. According to MOST, the bulk of R&D expenditure has been allocated to the high-tech industry. R&D funds are distributed to SOEs, local governments, and Chinese-owned firms. The 2004–2008 five-year plan calls for increased subsidies to SOEs (MOST 2006, table 5.2). Support for local government is targeted at the cities that house R&D centers within industrial parks. Local governments often match national government funding for R&D programs.

In short, China's high-tech promotion strategy had two prongs: build up capabilities of domestic firms and stimulate investment and technology transfer by MNCs. The results of China's high-tech program have been impressive. By 1989, the Legend group had evolved into Legend Computer and formed a joint venture with Hewlett Packard. By 2000, Legend had emerged as the number one seller of personal computers in the Asia Pacific region and held more than 20 percent of the Chinese PC market. In early 2005, Legend, which had morphed into Lenovo, acquired IBM's global desktop and notebook computer divisions. With the IBM deal, Lenovo became, after Dell and HP, the world's third largest PC maker (Spooner 2005). Hassee Computer is another fast-growing domestic computer firm. Domestic manufacturers together have dominated 70 percent of the Chinese market for PC sales (Walsh 2003, 108). Founder became a leading firm in developing laser typesetting technologies and electronic publishing. Datang is the leading company in the development of 3G (TD-SCDMA) technology. Huawei is a giant producer of telecommunication equipment. A collection of several domestic firms developed their own brand of mobile telephones and high-definition disc players. Table 6.5 exhibits a few other Chinese firms, including lesser-known ones that have made significant innovations.

Despite numerous problems at the beginning, particularly the lack of recognition of their capabilities and the relative merits of their product by Chinese customers, these domestic firms succeeded in penetrating into the internal and international market. They were highly encouraged to develop "leading technologies and leading products," focused on a

TABLE 6.5 Leading Innovative Domestic High-Tech Companies in China

Company Name	Founding	Major Technical Achievements
Huawel Technology	1988	Large-scale switch systems Next-generation network Optimal network Data communication
Shenzhen Zhongxin Technology Co.	1985	Large-scale switch systems Next-generation network TD-SCDMA
Datang Telecom Technology	1998	TD-SCDMA SCDMA
Dawning Information Industry Co.	1995	wormhole routing chip Parallel optimizing compiler Scalability, usability, manageability, and availability (SUMA) tech
Beijing Genome Institute	2002	Large-scale genome sequencing
Sibiono Gene Technology	1998	gene therapy medication for head and neck squamos cell carcinoma
China National Petroleum Co.	1955 (1988)	Integrated seismic data-processing software ABS technology Top-drive drilling equipment Multibranch horizontal and large displacement well-drilling tech Two-state catalytic cracking technology

SOURCE: Fan, Gao, and Watanabe (2007).

single product, collaborated with leading local providers of equipment and components, sought cooperation with MNCs, and collaborated with their customers. Government support was integral throughout the process (Gao et al. 2007).

Overall, by 2003, China's electronics sector generated $142 billion in exports and employed 4 million workers. Between 1993 and 2003, the growth rate of high-tech exports was 50.2 percent for computers and peripherals and 21.9 percent for telecommunications and related equipment.

Like Lenovo, many Chinese firms started as state-owned enterprises (SOEs) and were gradually privatized as they gained capacity and competitiveness. In 1993, 26 percent of computer and peripheral firms and 54 percent of telecommunications firms were SOEs. By 2003, only 6 percent of computer firms and 18 percent of telecom firms were SOEs.

Although national firms, including SOEs, are in the minority, they are filing and being granted more patent applications than foreign firms. According to MOST, Chinese firms were granted 112,103 patents in 2002, whereas foreign firms were granted only 20,296. Close to half of these patents were in the form of utility models—patents for incremental innovations where local firms create variations on project and process execution. This reveals that a significant amount of learning is going on in Chinese firms. Another half of the patents granted, however, are in the form of design patents, which totaled 49,143 in 2002 (MOST 2006).

Summary

It is clear from the analysis in this chapter that Mexico and China have followed very different policies for acquiring technological capabilities and bolstering industrialization. Mexico was the "champion of liberalization" but China's may be described as neo-developmental -evocative but not a clean replication of the NIC developmental states (see: ECLAC 2001). Alongside reform, China put in place functional and targeted government policies.

Perhaps more importantly, we have shown how Mexico's was a policy of dismantling a past set of policies and China's was a strategy of building new policies for the future. Mexico knew where it wanted to be and thought it had an easy way to get there: dismantle the old policies, and learning and growth would follow. China also had the same goal but was more modest about how to achieve it. China has implemented a two-pronged policy. While reforming the economy, it has taken a more gradual and experimental approach to liberalization and integration into the world economy. Meanwhile, it has continued a parallel set of targeted policies in support of development of indigenous capabilities for technological learning.

As early as 1990, the Mexican government relinquished all interference in the technology process, leaving it entirely to the parties involved in FDI. MNCs were also provided various incentives, particularly in export processing zones, without having to meet performance commitments. Economic liberalism also led to a reduction in government investment in R&D, education, and training. The assumption was that the market forces would take care of these issues.

Through trial and error, China has learned that reliance on market forces and FDI alone will not automatically lead to the transfer of technology and increase value-added in exports. There was a need for developing the capabilities of domestic firms. While formulating and implementing a comprehensive but selective and targeted strategy aimed in particular at high-tech industries, the government elaborated an institutional framework for S&T development and a dynamic national system of innovation. It consisted of the Chinese Academy of Science, relevant ministries, private enterprises, universities, and research institutes. Close links were established among these entities in the public and private sectors. Both basic research and application and diffusion of technology have been emphasized from the early 1980s.

Up until 1984, LAC's industrial policy—manifested by the Mexican example—was geared to intervene strongly in specific sectors. Since then, policy has been to let markets largely determine the profile of manufacturing and exports.

China's rise poses real challenges for Latin American economic development. Yet the moment can be seen as an opportunity as well. The rapid accumulation of industrial competitiveness and subsequent growth in China is a signal to LAC that another path is still possible in the twenty-first century.

In this book we have examined the extent to which China's unprecedented economic expansion has affected the economies of LAC. In so doing, we focused in the first chapter on the bilateral trade relationship between LAC and China. We analyzed the extent to which China's rise has impacted demand for LAC exports, and we looked at the composition of those exports. In the next two chapters, we examined how LAC manufactures exporters are faring in the competition with their Chinese counterparts in world and regional markets. We then analyzed specifically the competition between Mexico and China in the U.S. market. Finally, in the last chapter, we conducted a comparative analysis of government policy regarding industrial innovation and competitiveness in China and Mexico. Four major findings stem from our work:

1) LAC exports to China are heavily concentrated in a handful of countries and sectors, leaving the majority of LAC without the opportunity to significantly gain from China as a market for their exports.

In Chapter 2 we show that in the rise in China trade from LAC, the majority of all exports to China are clustered in six primary-product commodities housed in just ten LAC countries. Current signs show that Chinese demand for these products is here to stay for the foreseeable future. Yet in the long run, prices and demand for these types of commodities tend to decline. Furthermore, while much attention has been given to the fact that LAC exports to China have increased, imports from China have increased faster and may pose longer-run current-account problems. Finally, given that LAC nations have yet to create the necessary level of environmental institutions, our research suggests that the China-led demand for primary commodities may lead to costly environmental problems for LAC and the world in terms of deforestation's impact on global climate change.

For the handful of LAC nations and the sectors within them that have significantly expanded due to China, the picture is more positive—at least it was. China's growth has affected the world price of many other exports that LAC offers the world. This result, in turn, has led to an overall increase in exports and foreign exchange for the LAC region. Moreover, some of the nations in LAC have learned from past mistakes and now have in place stabilization funds that allowed them to store reserves. These reserves put LAC in a much better position to recover from the economic crisis and place their economies on a more competitive path.

2) China is increasingly outcompeting LAC manufactures exports in world and regional markets, and the worst may be yet to come.

In Chapters 3 and 4 we examine evidence of the current and potential ability of China to outcompete LAC in world and regional manufacturing markets. World manufactures export markets have been the most dynamic part of the world economy, growing more than sixfold since the 1980s. China's and LAC's exports both grew even more than the world average during that period. Since 2000, however, we find that, market by market, China's penetration of world manufacturing markets is exceptionally faster and deeper than LAC's on almost any count. Indeed, we find that 94 percent of all LAC manufacturing exports are under threat from China. That 94 percent comprises 40 percent of all LAC's exports. LAC countries are also losing their foothold in their own region and are being all but left behind in high-tech trade in the world economy. The most recent work that compares export similarity between LAC countries and China shows that these trends are likely to continue, at least for countries like Argentina, Brazil, Chile, and Mexico.

In Chapter 4 we look even more closely at the competitiveness of LAC's high-technology exports in relation to China. This chapter shows that not many LAC nations have put together much technological capability at all, but those that have are threatened by China in world markets. We discover that China went from having practically no high-technology export activity in the 1980s to being the most competitive high-tech exporter in the world. More than one in ten high-technology products sold in world markets come from mainland China. In terms of competitiveness with LAC, we find that 95 percent of all of LAC's high-tech exports are under threat from China, representing close to 12 percent of all LAC exports.

We then, in Chapter 5, zero in on Mexico and confirm work in earlier studies that shows how at present how Mexico is the hardest hit. We focus on China and Mexico in the U.S. market, Mexico's most important, where 85 percent of its exports are destined, where 50 percent of its imports come from. We find that 80 percent of Mexico's exports are under threat in the U.S. market. This is most disturbing given the vast geographical differences in proximity in Mexico versus China, and the fact that through NAFTA, Mexico enjoys vastly better access to U.S. market in terms of tariffs and preferences.

3) **China is rapidly building the technological capabilities necessary for industrial development, whereas LAC (and particularly Mexico) is not paying enough attention to innovation and industrial development.**

In Chapter 6 we conducted a comparative analysis of the role of government policies in industrial learning and the development of capabilities of indigenous firms in Mexico and China in order to shed light on why China is outperforming Mexico. We find that Mexico and China have had starkly different approaches to economic reform in this area. Mexico has followed a "neoliberal" path, whereas China's approach could be described as "neodevelopmental." Mexico's hands-off approach to learning has resulted in a lack of development of endogenous capacity of domestic firms, little transfer of technology, negligible progress in the upgrading of industrial production, and little increase in value added of exports. By contrast, China has deployed a hands-on approach of targeting and nurturing domestic firms through a gradual and trial-and-error led set of government policies.

4) **These three trends could accentuate a pattern of specialization in LAC that could hurt LAC's longer-run prospects for economic development.**

The overreliance on primary commodities exports was a trend that plagued LAC for much of the nineteenth and twentieth centuries. From 1940 and almost through the 1980s, LAC began to build some technological and industrial capabilities that put it on a path toward global competitiveness. The twin trends of LAC's being drawn further into primary commodities (following Chinese demand and the incentives of indirect price effects due to China's rise), while simultaneously beginning to lose its grip in world and regional manufactures markets, threaten to strip away a half century of progress toward industrial development in LAC.

Need for More Research

This book is far from the last word on this subject. Indeed, as a very short amount of time has unfolded, the same methodologies have yielded very different results. Early work on export structure and on relative competitiveness showed that China was not much of a potential threat to LAC. That completely changed with just a few more years of data. In addition to needing more time to analyze these trends, there is complementary work that needs to be done as well.

One aspect of the China-LAC economic relationship has received glaringly little attention—the impact of China trade on domestic firms in LAC markets. To what extent are China's exports to LAC affecting production and employment in the manufacturing sector? The answer to this question could go in two directions. On the one hand, if the surge in China exports to LAC occurs as inputs to LAC firms that make such firms more competitive (given the cheaper price of inputs), then China exports to LAC could be a net benefit. On the other hand, Chinese exports could be displacing many firms in LAC's domestic markets. Such analyses would have to weigh benefits to consumers versus the long-run economy-wide effects of the results.

Another area that needs more research is whether in the long run China-LAC trade will cause resource curse and environmental problems for LAC. As discussed in Chapter 2, resource curses can occur when exports-demand increases for commodities cause exchange-rate appreciation and therefore can crowd out the competitiveness of noncommodity sectors such as manufacturing. If Chinese demand and the impact of that demand on overall world prices continues to lead to a surge in LAC commodities exports, a careful eye on the part of scholars and policymakers will be needed. What's more, the environmental effects of primary commodities exploitation, especially in the soy, meat, and mining sectors, can be considerable. New research should be devised to examine the extent to which China-led trade is affecting the environment in LAC.

Finally, surprisingly little work has been done on the extent to which China can be an export (and or investment) opportunity for noncommodity LAC exporters. Currently, we find that China is not now importing much in the way of manufactures, especially from LAC. However, as China continues to develop it will demand an increasing array of consumer goods. Further analysis is needed to see what niche markets in China's mammoth economy can serve as opportunities for LAC.

Lessons for Policy

The findings in this book suggest that policy discussions regarding economic development in LAC need to be elevated to a high-priority level (Wise and Quiliconi 2007; Hogenboom 2009). In so doing, it will be easy and tempting to look backward to the period roughly between 1940 and 1970. During that period LAC was indeed able to build innovation and industrial capabilities. Indeed, that period was certainly the "golden age" of economic growth in LAC that is yet to be matched. However, the world economy has changed significantly, and what worked—somewhat—in the past is rarely a recipe for the future. One feature of LAC's golden age was that there was an anti-export bias with manufactures. Building domestic demand is a vital part of any development strategy, but relying exclusively on it is another thing. That was a mistake made by LAC and one of the reasons so many of its industries fell by the wayside in the 1980s and 1990s when markets were opened to foreign competition.

With these factors in mind, we draw three general lessons for policy that stem from our analysis:

1) Economic diversification and innovation for competitiveness should form the core of future discussions of economic policy in LAC.

We know that economic growth and a diversified economy go hand in hand. It is important to underscore "diversity" because past analyses have focused on moving away from primary commodity production rather than building upon and diversifying alongside commodity production. Hundreds of years show us that primary-commodities production is an asset that LAC can build upon. LAC needs to see to it that the proper environmental provisions are put in place so that LAC can maintain its foothold in commodities markets for years to come. LAC also needs to refocus on the competitiveness of products beyond primary commodities.

Diversification strategies will take different forms in different LAC countries. In contrast with the past, it will be more important for LAC countries to put in place a process of industrial policy, as opposed to policies themselves. Past attempts at industrialization in the region had a one-size-fits-all approach: industrialize in all sectors at all costs. New, more nuanced approaches to industrial policy emphasize the need to put in place a process whereby policymakers (embedded within the private sector) can "self-discover" the binding constraints to economic growth in a particular economy. After such a "diagnostic" approach is in place, the policy process can commence (Rodrik 2007).

2) Building the capabilities for industrial competitiveness is a long-run process that will take consistent leadership and accountability on the part of governments and the private sector.

One aspect of economic policy in LAC that has become abundantly clear over the past fifty years is that the political economy of economic policy is just as important as the policies themselves. Government efforts to play a role in economic diversification have been rightly criticized on the grounds that government failures can be rife. Two of the most salient criticisms are that governments do not have the proper expertise to correctly diagnose an economy, and that when engaging in the policy process, governments can be prey to rent-seeking behavior.

Because of the risk of government failure, it is of the utmost importance to have a high degree of government leadership and accountability—mechanisms utilized by the most successful East Asian economies (Amsden 2001). First, leadership is needed to take the long-run view on economic development because there may not be much of a domestic political constituency for diversification policies in the short run. Many of the beneficiaries of a diversification strategy—producers that could emerge from successful policies, and longer-run consumer welfare beneficiaries—are presently weak or do not even exist yet! Second, to avoid problems of inadequately "picking winners," governments will need to be embedded within the private sector during growth diagnostics so they get the right signals.

These policies need to be coupled with accountability measures in order to work. First, governments need to put conditionalities on the private sector in the form of performance requirements. Firms and sectors will need to show that they are making demonstrable progress on technological development and innovation in order to maintain support. Finally, mechanisms of government accountability need to be in place to cut down on rent seeking.

3) LAC and other developing nations need the policy space in international commitments to discover the proper path for economic development in their respective countries.

China and other East Asian nations have been and continue to be the most successful industrializers and globalizers in the world economy. East Asia has enjoyed a great deal more policy space than most of the nations in LAC have. A majority of LAC nations have made it more difficult to deploy the proper policies to loosen the binding constraints on their economies for three reasons. First, there was a paradigmatic ideological shift toward the Washington Consensus within LAC that led many nations to unilaterally pursue now discredited policy. Second, their own macroeconomic mismanagement in the 1980s and 1990s meant they needed to seek help from the International Monetary Fund and the World Bank, which at the time considerably frowned upon active government support of economic diversification. Finally, many LAC nations have signed bilateral and regional preferential trade agreements (PTAs) with the United States and Europe (Denae Thrasher and Gallagher 2008) that further constrain the policy space for industrial policy and lock it in.

Until 1997 East Asian nations did not need to go to the IMF and World Bank for help and were able to avoid the more draconian conditionalities that go with loans from these institutions. Moreover, most East Asian nations (until very recently) have shied away from PTAs in favor of the more flexible WTO, where many of the more appropriate policies are still permitted. It is not surprising that Argentina and Brazil, two of the more industrialized nations in LAC, have also steered cleared from PTAs in favor of the WTO and have rushed to repay their outstanding loans with the IMF. LAC as a whole would be better off to follow that lead.

Crisis as Opportunity

In 2008 the world economy experienced a marked financial crisis like none other since the early 1900s. In response to the crisis, many countries are taking the opportunity to retool their economies. In addition to stimulating aggregate demand and bailing out banking systems, some countries are seizing this opportunity to simultaneously bolster the productive capacities of their economies. That is certainly the case in China and to some extent the United States. With a handful of exceptions, LAC has not seized this opportunity. There is still time.

Both China and LAC had a big role to play in the crisis. In response to the United States' post–September 11 recession, the United States engaged in expansionary monetary and fiscal policy in the form of interest-rate and tax cuts alongside increases in public spending. Not long thereafter, in a period of massive liquidity due in part to the lower interest rates and income growth, the United States experienced a housing boom. "Innovators" in financial services firms collateralized the mortgage loans going into these homes and securitized them into numerous hedge funds, credit default swaps, and other financial instruments (after they were stamped with AAA ratings from the credit-rating agencies). China fueled this process by purchasing government debt so as to keep its pegged exchange rate relatively cheap in terms of the U.S. dollar. This action enabled China's industrial exports to surge into the pockets of debt-ridden consumers in the United States. China's growth from this process fueled increases in demand, much of it in the form of primary commodities from LAC. As this process ensued over the decade, China and LAC accumulated a massive amount of reserves (China from purchasing debt, LAC from net exports of commodities), and the United States accumulated a correspondingly high level of debt. When the U.S. housing market started to decline, U.S. consumers were not able to pay their debts to the banking system—a banking system that had spread these mortgages thin and across the entire world economy. Thus, the underlying assets that formed the core of so many investments became "toxic."

We all know what happened after that. Credit seized, and the world economy faltered. In response to the crisis, economists and policymakers converged (for the first time on these issues in close to thirty years) around the idea that the binding constraints to recovery were aggregate demand and bank liquidity. Many nations in the world aggressively engaged in countercyclical and expansionary fiscal and monetary policies. Countries around the world have supplied trillions of dollars to their banking systems in hopes that credit would resume. In terms of fiscal policy, in early 2009 the United States began disbursing a fiscal stimulus package of upwards of $700 billion or 5.5 percent of GDP. About 6 percent of that stimulus package goes to the building of new environmentally friendly technologies such as renewable energy, clean cars, and a new electricity grid for the United States.

China's reaction was also strong. China's fiscal stimulus package was over $500 billion, but it represents an astonishing 12.5 percent of GDP. According to Keith Bradsher of the *New York Times* (2009a) China used " its nearly $600 billion economic stimulus package to make its companies better able to compete in markets at home and abroad, to retrain migrant workers on an immense scale and to rapidly expand subsidies for research and development." What's more, according to Bradsher, 12 percent of China's $500 billion stimulus package is climate-friendly. China will be spending stimulus funds on high-speed rail, low-carbon car production, renewable energy, and energy-efficient buildings. China already leads the world in installed renewable energy capacity with forty-two gigawatts of capacity (compared to twenty-three in the United States) (Bradsher 2009b).

Latin America was among the regions of the developing world hardest-hit by the crisis—though it was not as hard-hit as it had been during past crises. According to a comprehensive analysis by Ocampo (2009), LAC was affected by the crisis in three areas. First and foremost, the contraction in global demand after the crisis hit has hurt LAC exporters, especially manufacturing exporters in Mexico and Central America. Commodities exporters in South America were hurt as well, as demand losses decreased the prices of commodities and deflated the commodities boom. In terms of finance, it is true that LAC avoided many of the toxic assets that eroded the developed world's financial systems. The region had accumulated significant reserves that proved useful in defending their currencies—which have not been as hard-hit as during the crises of the 1980s and 1990s. However, the one area where significant strife is located is in corporate debt. Many LAC companies borrowed heavily to finance expansion, in dollars. As the crisis has hit, these firms suffer from both a lack of demand and an increase in debt. Finally, though least significantly, says Ocampo, a decline in remittances to LAC from higher-income countries has been a key transmitter of the crisis as well.

Again, Mexico is an exception. Mexico has been among the worst-hit by the crisis. As we showed in Chapter 5, Mexico has hung its hat on the U.S. economy, with more than 80 percent of all Mexican exports destined for the United States. Given the shrinking of U.S. demand during the crisis, Mexico contracted significantly. Industrial production declined by over 10 percent in 2009, and GDP as a whole was projected to shrink by 7.1 percent despite the frantic effort to save the economy. Indeed, lack of demand for Mexican products caused a 40 percent decline in the value of the peso. Mexico's central bank spent close to $30 billion of its reserves to save the peso since the crisis hit. According to Bloomberg News, Mexico sold $50 million daily and $250 million (to buy pesos) when the peso weakened more than 2 percent in a day. CEMEX, the only LAC company among the top MNCs in the world economy that expanded during the boom years, in part from dollar-denominated debt, now is contracting severely and selling plants across the world. Given that many Mexicans worked in the U.S. market as carpenters and landscapers connected to the housing boom, that bust has meant a major contraction in remittances as well.

Despite China's apparent focus on boosting domestic demand, during 2009 it continued to anchor its currency to the U.S. dollar, keeping

China's exports cheap. Indeed, China financed a significant portion of the U.S. stimulus effort. During the later part of 2009, amid concerns of growing U.S. debt, many investors that had originally sought refuge in the dollar began looking elsewhere—and there was a massive return in capital flows to some LAC nations, which caused significant appreciation in currencies in some places. Brazil saw a 35 percent appreciation in its currency relative to the dollar during the fall of 2009 and had to resort to capital controls to try to stem the bubble. These trends put LAC at a further disadvantage vis-à-vis China.

On the other hand, compared to past crises, it is amazing that LAC has been able to respond positively at all to this crisis. With the exception of Mexico, most nations across the hemisphere did not need to run to the international financial institutions for help. According to the United Nations Economic Commission for Latin America and the Caribbean (CEPAL), virtually every nation in LAC has adopted some form of countercyclical response to the crisis in the form of monetary or fiscal expansion (ECLAC 2009). That being said, the relative size of the LAC response and the composition of such efforts leaves a lot to be desired. The largest stimulus package in LAC was undertaken by Chile, at 2.5 percent of GDP. As discussed in Chapter 2, this was enabled by Chile's innovative funds created from high commodities prices. Countries such as Mexico that were much harder hit are doing far less. Some countries such as Brazil have used some of their efforts toward research and development and diversification. Brazil capitalized its national development bank, BNDES, with significant funds to continue programs to that end.

Beyond the immediate response to the crisis, there is still plenty of time to rethink and retool economic policy in LAC. Although growth picked up in 2009–10 in the world economy, markets were still very timid. In many ways, that is good news in disguise for LAC, because it may not immediately face cutthroat competition overseas or import penetration at home. Rather than pointing fingers outside the region for LAC's development woes, the crisis can spark an internal stock-taking to conduct a thorough diagnosis of the binding constraints that hold LAC economies back. This breathing room will not last forever. China continues to provide support in terms of exchange-rate policy and capacity building to its export sector.

It is time to confront the dragon in the room. This book has shown that LAC cannot ride the coattails of China's growth through exporting to China. Moreover, and worse still, if LAC does not increase its industrial competitiveness, China can take many of LAC's markets across the globe, and at home. This could be devastating. As we have shown, LAC relies on regional and world markets for a vast portion of its current level of diversification. Receding from that could put the region back on a resource-dependent path. This could be further accentuated in the handful of countries that also see surges in resource-based exports to China.

Rather than a discussion of how to combat China, a regional discussion about industrialization should seek to learn from China. No other developing country has achieved such notable changes in industrial structure, changes that are far from complete. China, of course, is not a case that can be cut and pasted into LAC development strategies. Only Brazil, and to a lesser extent Mexico, have the manufacturing capabilities, export markets, and domestic markets to try to mimic the scale of Chinese activity. However, in some manner, both of these countries did try a similar approach to China in the 1950s through the 1970s, with only limited success. For the remainder of the region, nations might want to look to some of China's neighbors, such as Malaysia, Thailand, and Taiwan, to examine how they can serve niches that complement China as it emerges significant in global-value chains.

At the very least, the findings in this book should spark a pragmatic discussion of the role of technology and industry in twenty-first century economic development. Twentieth century LAC was plagued by extremes in terms of economic policy. During the early part of the century, LAC engaged in heavy-handed economic policy that had some gains but eventually ran its course. The latter part of the century was characterized by a complete pendulum swing to what one might call free market fundamentalism. Though not without its successes as well, the Washington Consensus has largely failed in LAC. What is needed is a pragmatic approach that must include a discussion of the role of technology, innovation, and industry. Economic theory tells us that nations with a more diversified economy grow faster and are more stable.

LAC is going in the opposite direction, in part accentuated by China's rise. It is time for policymakers and business people to forge a balanced approach to economic development where the state helps foster an environment in which the private market can thrive and compete. LAC is promising because it still has a considerable manufacturing base from which it can build. Thanks in part to China, it also is in a better fiscal and monetary position than it has been since before the 1980s.

LAC stands with an opportunity to put its development problems behind it in the twenty-first century. If the opportunity is not seized, the fault, dear Brutus, will not be in the stars.

Technical Appendix

A. General Methodology

For the majority of the calculations in this book, we use trade data from the United Nations Statistics Division's "Commodity Trade Statistics Database" (COMTRADE), the gold standard for trade data. Indeed, unless indicated otherwise one can assume that all trade data discussed in this volume comes from COMTRADE. We download data at the three-digit level, following the second revision of the SITC classification.

We classify the data into "commodities," "manufacturing," and "high tech," using Sanjaya Lall's "Technological Classification of Exports" developed in (Lall 2000) (see table A.1). In "commodities" we group all products in the PP, RB1, and RB2 categories; in "manufacturing" we group all products in LT1, LT2, MT1, MT2, MT3, HT1, and HT2; and in "high technology" we group all products in HT1 and HT2. Therefore, "manufacturing" includes "high-tech" products.

B. Threat Analyses

To measure changes in competitiveness, we follow the approach developed by Lall and Weiss (Lall and Weiss 2005). (Sometimes we use this approach with minor variations. We outline in the pages that follow, when necessary, the specific calculations conducted for different tables.)

TABLE A.1   Classification of Technology Levels in the World Economy

PP	Primary products
RB1	Resource-based manufactures: Agro-based
RB2	Resource-based manufactures: Other
LT1	Low-technology manufactures: Textiles, garments, and footware
LT2	Low-technology manufactures: Other products
MT1	Medium-technology manufactures: Automotive
MT2	Medium-technology manufactures: Process
MT3	Medium-technology manufactures: Engineering
HT1	High-technology manufactures: Electronic and electrical
HT2	High-technology manufactures: Other

SOURCE: Lall (2000).

Lall and Weiss look at the evolution of China and LAC export shares in both the world and U.S. markets and look for evidence of increased Chinese competition in products that show increased penetration of Chinese exports in coincidence with decreased penetration of LAC exports.[1]

As shown in table A.2, Lall and Weiss define a category in which China's market share is rising and LAC's decreasing for the U.S. market as a category in which LAC is experiencing a "direct threat" from China. Similarly, they define a category in which both China's and LAC's shares are increasing, but China's share is increasing faster, as a category in which LAC is experiencing a "partial threat" from China.

We call the difference in market shares between two periods of time "dynamic revealed comparative position" or DRCP.

C. Calculating Changes in Market Shares

For table 3.2 (Chapter 3) and tables 4.3 and 4.4 (Chapter 4), we calculate market shares and DRCPs as a country's exports to the world for a given year and product, divided by the sum of all the countries in the world's exports to the world for the same year and product (which we label "world exports"). In this, we depart from Lall and Weiss, as they calculate market shares in the U.S. market, and we do it for the world market as a whole.

TABLE A.2 Framework for Threat Analysis

		Chinese Export Market Shares	
		Rising	*Falling*
Other countries' export market shares	Rising	**A. *No threat*** Both countries have rising market shares, and the latter is gaining more than China. **B. *Partial threat*** Both are gaining market share, but China is gaining faster than the other country.	**C. *Reverse threat*** No competitive threat from China. The threat is the reverse, from the other country to China.
	Falling	**D. *Direct threat*** China gains market share and the other country. This may indicate causal connection unless the country was loses. This losing market share in the absence of Chinese entry.	**E. *Mutual withdrawal: No threat*** Both parties lose market shares in export markets to other competitors.

SOURCE: Lall and Weiss (2005).

More specifically, the DRCP is calculated as follows for country j in sector i between the years y_1 and y_2:

$$DRCP_{j,i,y_1-y_2} = \left(\frac{X_{j,i,y_2}}{\sum\limits_{j} X_{j,i,y_2}} - \frac{X_{j,i,y_1}}{\sum\limits_{j} X_{j,i,y_1}} \right) * 100$$

where the nominator, X_{j,i,y_2}, represents exports of country (j) in sector (i) in year y_2, and the denominator, $\sum\limits_{j} X_{j,i,y_2}$, represents world exports for the same sector (i) in the same year y_2.

For tables 3.2 (Chapter 3) we conduct this for all products in the "manufacturing" category, and for and tables 4.3 and 4.4 (Chapter 4) only for the products in the "high-tech" categories.

For tables 3.3 and 3.4 (Chapter 3), we calculate market shares and DRCPs as Latin American imports from a given country for a given year and product, divided by Latin America imports from the world for the same year and product. Again, in this case we depart from Lall and Weiss, as they calculate market shares in the U.S. market, and we do it for the Latin American import market.

More specifically, we use the following formula for analyzing the Chinese threat to any Latin American country (x) in Latin American markets:

$$DRCP_{x,y,z_1-z_2} = \left(\frac{(LACM - x)_{x,y,z_2}}{(LACM - x)_{World,y,z_2}} - \frac{(LACM - x)_{x,y,z_1}}{(LACM - x)_{World,y,z_1}} \right) * 100$$

And we compare it with China's, which we calculate as:

$$DRCP_{China,y,z_1-z_2} = \left(\frac{(LACM - x)_{China,y,z_2}}{(LACM - x)_{World,y,z_2}} - \frac{(LACM - x)_{China,y,z_1}}{(LACM - x)_{World,y,z_1}} \right) * 100$$

where $(LACM - x)$ represents LAC imports (calculated as the sum of the imports to all countries in Latin America, except country x) from country x in sector y, in year z. We exclude country x when calculating the level of LAC imports because, while it is obvious that country x will not import from itself, it may import from China. For the comparison to be meaningful, we need to look at export performance in the same market. In this case, that market is "the rest of LAC" as viewed from the perspective of the country under study.

More specifically, for services the DRCP is calculated as follows for country j in sector i between the years y_1 and y_2:

$$DRCP_{j,i,y_1-y_2} = \left(\frac{XS_{j,i,y_2}}{\sum\limits_{j} XS_{j,i,y_2}} - \frac{XS_{j,i,y_1}}{\sum\limits_{j} XS_{j,i,y_1}} \right) * 100$$

Where the nominator, XS_{j,i,y_2}, represents total exports of services country j in sector i in year y_2 and the denominator, $\sum\limits_{j} XS_{j,i,y_2}$, represents world exports of total services for the same sector i in the same year y_2.

Finally, when we look specifically at the case of Mexico in Tables 5.1, 5.2, and 5.3 (Chapter 5), we follow Lall and Weiss's analysis more closely, looking exclusively at competitiveness in the U.S. market, from the perspective of U.S. imports (as opposed to Mexican and Chinese exports to the United States). More specifically, we measure the DRCP as:

$$DRCP_{j,i,y_1-y_2} = \left(\frac{USM_{j,i,y_2}}{\sum_j USM_{j,i,y_2}} - \frac{USM_{j,i,y_1}}{\sum_j USM_{j,i,y_1}} \right) * 100$$

where the nominator, USM_{j,i,y_2}, represents U.S. imports from country j—in this case, only Mexico and China—in sector i in year y_2 and the denominator, $\sum_j USM_{j,i,y_2}$, represents the sum of all U.S. imports for all countries for the same sector i in the same year y_2.

D. Additional Calculations to Chapter 5: Speed and Acceleration Analyses

One aspect not discussed in Chapter 5 due to its perhaps overly technical nature is relative speed of changes in market share exhibited by China and Mexico. For calculating the speed, we calculated every country in the world's share of world exports in *manufacturing* for every year between 1985 and 2006 (henceforth, *manufacturing* market share). We then calculated the "speed of change in competitiveness" for every pair of years (1986–1985, 1987–1986, and so on) by subtracting the *manufacturing* market share of the earlier year from the *manufacturing* market share of the latter year. While speed is usually calculated by dividing a change in position by a time frame (for example, miles per hour), this is not necessary in our case because we are looking at single-year intervals (and we would have to divide by one.)

More specifically, the speed of change in competitiveness for country X between years A and $A-1$ is calculated as follows:

$$Speed_{X,A,A-1} = \frac{Exports_{X,A}}{Exports_{World,A}} - \frac{Exports_{X,A-1}}{Exports_{World,A-1}}$$

The results of this calculation are presented in Figure A.1:

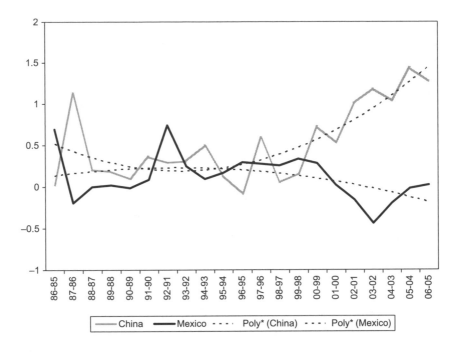

FIGURE A.1   Speed of Changes in Manufacturing Market Share
SOURCE: Author's calculations based on United Nations Statistics Division (2009).
*POLY=Polynomial trend line (second degree).

Three elements are important to highlight about Figure A.1. First, so long as the full lines are above the zero line, a country's share of world exports is increasing. For most of the period (1985–2006), both Mexico and China are, for the most part, increasing their manufacturing market share (with a brief exception for China in 1995–1996 and for Mexico in 1987–1988 and a not so brief exception for Mexico between 2001 and 2006). Second, it is important to look at the height of the line, which shows the actual magnitude of the increases (or decreases) in market share. As can be seen in Figure A.1, until 2001 there were years were China outpaced Mexico and years when Mexico outpaced China. Since 2001, however, China has dramatically outpaced Mexico, not only because Mexico moved into negative territory but, perhaps more importantly, because China's pace of market-share growth picked up speed.

This leads us to the final important point worth highlighting. The dotted lines represent the trend lines (as second-degree polynomial functions of the form $y = ax^2 + b$), and their slopes represent the change in speed, otherwise known as acceleration. What is patently clear from Figure A.1 is not only that China is gaining market share at a higher speed than Mexico, but also that every year that goes by—because of the positive acceleration of market-share changes—it gains speed at a higher and higher rate.

Notes

Chapter 1

1. The focus of this book is entirely on the economic relationship between China and Latin America. For a broader analysis that includes foreign policy implications, see Domínguez (2006).

Chapter 2

1. A more detailed analysis of Argentinean trade with China, where the importance of soy is made extremely clear, has been conducted by López and Ramos (2007).

2. The reason why this percentage can exceed 100 is that Table 2.4 actually divides the *change* in Chinese import demand by the *change* in world exports. Even though Chinese imports could never exceed world exports, in some cases the growth in Chinese imports exceeds the growth in world exports as a result of a reduction of imports in other markets.

Chapter 3

1. Where "a market share loss for LAC (in any product or market) is understood as a reflection of the fact that its exports have grown less than world exports because its exports were (1) less dynamic than those of China and/or (2) less dynamic than those of the rest of the world." Because he focuses on China, Mesquita Moreira's figures refer to "the losses due to (1), that is, market share losses that can be attributed directly to China, measured as a percentage of total exports in 2004" (Mesquita Moreira 2007).

Chapter 4

1. With respect to FDI, which we do not address in this book, the literature finds that with regard to trade and investment flows, China accounts for a significant amount of the boost in LAC exports and foreign investment in recent years, but is exporting more than it imports. (A thorough review of this literature is can be found in Jenkins, Dussel Peters, and Mesquita Moreira [2006]; and Gallagher, Moreno-Brid, and Porzecanski [2008]).

Chapter 5

1. In the last fifteen years, the flow of private banks' credit to production purposes has shrunk more than fifteen points as a proportion of GDP, and by 2005 this ratio was one of the lowest in Latin America.

2. In the late 1990s, among the large economies in Latin America, Mexico was the one with the lowest investment in infrastructure as a proportion of GDP (Calderón and Servén 2004).

Chapter 6

1. For more details on List's ideas, see: Shafaeddin 2005, particularly pp. 47–50).

2. See, for example, the reference in Bruton (1998, 930). There are at least two versions of the theory, TCB and Lazonick (1991). Lazonick's theory is concerned basically with large firms of developed countries and thus isnot discussed here.

3. For a good presentation and development of the theory, see Lall (1993).

4. For more details, see Pizarro and Shafaeddin (2007).

5. They were mainly located in Beijing, Shanghai, and Shenzhen. Of 33,392 high-tech enterprises, 67 percent were located in high-tech parks (Fan, Gao, and Watanabe 2007, 356).

6. These include Huawei, Shenzhen Zhongxin, Datang, Dawning, Beijing Genome Institutes, and China National Petroleum (see Fan, Gao, and Watanabe 2007).

7. (Based on People's Republic of China (2006, tables 21-13 and 21-9).

8. They include Intel, SAP, Motorola, Lucent, Turbolinux, Nokia, IBM, Ericsson, Agilent, Microsoft, Matsushita, NEC, and Samsung (Chen 2008, table A1).

9. For a brief history of development of the industry up to 1993, see Ye (2008).

Technical Appendix

1. Of course, the idea of measuring competitiveness by looking at different countries' market shares was first introduced by Balassa (1965), and Lall and

Weiss's approach builds on this idea. In a 1965 paper, Balassa introduced this concept to empirically measure the competitiveness of different countries. The revealed comparative advantage for sector i in country j was defined as follows:

$$RCA_{ij} = \frac{X_{ij} / \sum_i X_{ij}}{\sum_j X_{ij} / \sum_i \sum_j X_{ij}}$$

The numerator represents the share that any given sector (i) represents of national exports of any given country j. The denominator represents the percentage share of the same sector in OECD exports. Therefore, the RCA is a comparison between the export structure of any given country and the export structure of the OECD as a whole. When the RCA is greater than one for any given sector, then the country being analyzed is said to be specialized in that sector, and vice versa when the RCA is smaller than 1 (Laursen 1998).

Bibliography

Agosin, Manuel, and Roberto Machado. 2005. Foreign Investment in Developing Countries: Does It Crowd in Domestic Investment? *Oxford Development Studies* 33 (2):149–162.

Álvarez, Roberto, and Sebastián Claro. 2009. David *Versus* Goliath: The Impact of Chinese Competition on Developing Countries. *World Development* 37 (3): 560–571.

Amsden, Alice. 2001. *The Rise of the "Rest": Challenges to the West From Late-Industrializing Economies*. Oxford: Oxford University Press.

Amsden, Alice H., and Wan-wen Chu. 2003. *Beyond Late Development: Taiwan's Upgrading Policies*. Cambridge, MA: MIT Press.

Archibugi, D., and M. Michi. 1997. Technological Globalization or National System of Innovation? *Futures* 29 (2):121–137.

Arrow, K. J. 1962. The Economic Implications of Learning by Doing. *Review of Economic Studies* 29 (3):155–173.

Baer, Werner. 1971. The Role of Government Enterprises in Latin America's Industrialization. In *Fiscal Policy for Industrialization and Development in Latin America*, ed. David T. Geithman. Gainesville: University Press of Florida.

Balassa, Bela. 1965. Trade Liberalization and "Revealed" Comparative Advantage. *Manchester School of Economics and Social Studies* 32:99–123.

Baldwin, R.E. 1969. The Case Against Infant-Industry Tariff Protection. *Journal of Political Economy* 77 (3):295–305.

Banco de México. 2006. Estadísticas (http://www.banxico.org.mx/tipo/estadisticas/index.html), Mexico City, Bank of Mexico.

Barbier, Edward B. 2004. Agricultural Expansion, Resource Booms and Growth in Latin America: Implications for Long-Run Economic Development. *World Development* 32 (1):137–157.

Bell, M., B. Ross-Larson, and L. E. Westphal. 1984. Assessing the Performance of Infant Industries. *Journal of Development Economics* 16:101–128.

Blázquez-Lidoy, Jorge, Javier Rodríguez, and Javier Santiso. 2006. Angel or Devil? China's Trade Impact on Latin American Emerging Markets. *CEPAL Review* 90: 15–41.

Bradsher, Keith. 2009a. China Grows More Picky About Debt. *New York Times*, May 20, http://www.nytimes.com/2009/05/21/business/global/21reserves.html?_r=1&pagewanted=1.

———. 2009b. As China Stirs Economy, Some See Protectionism. *New York Times*, June 23, http://www.nytimes.com/2009/06/24/business/economy/24yuan.html.

Bruton, H. 1998. A Reconsideration of Import Substitution. *Journal of Economic Literature* 36:903–936.

CADELEC. 2004. Cadena Productiva de la Electronica 2004 *Available at www.cadalec.com.mx* [accessed April 2004].

Calderón, César. 2009. Trade, Specialization, and Cycle Synchronization: Explaining Output Comovement Between Latin America, China, and India. In *China's and India's Challenge to Latin America: Opportunity or Threat?*, ed. D. Lederman, M. Olarreaga, and G. E. Perry. Washington, DC: World Bank.

Calderón, César, and Luis Servén. 2004. *Trends in Infrastructure in Latin America, 1980–2001*. Santiago, Chile: Banco Central de Chile.

Carrillo, J., and A. Hualde. 2002. La maquiladora electronica en Tijuana: Hacia un cluster fronterizo. *Revista Mexicana de Sociologia* 64 (3):125–171.

Chen, Kun, and Martin Kenney. 2008. Universities/Research Institutes and Regional Innovation Systems: The Cases of Beijing and Shenzhen. *World Development* 35 (6):1056–1074.

Chen, Y. 2008. Why Do Multinational Corporations Locate Their Advanced R&D Centres in Beijing? *Journal of Development Studies* 44 (5):622–644.

China's Quest for Resources: A Ravenous Dragon. 2008. *Economist*, May 13. *Available at www.economist.com.*

Cimoli, Mario. 2000a. Conclusions: An Appreciative Pattern of the Mexican Innovation System. In *Developing Innovation Systems: Mexico in a Global Context*, ed. M. Cimoli. London and New York: Continuum.

———. 2000b. *Developing Innovation Systems: Mexico in Global Context*. New York and London: Continuum.

Cimoli, Mario, and Jorge Katz. 2003. Structural reforms, technological gaps and economic development: a Latin American perspective *Industrial and Corporate Change* 12 (2):387–411.

Clements, Benedict, Christopher Faircloth, and Marijn Verhoeven. 2007. Public Expenditure in Latin America: Trends and Key Policy Issues. *CEPAL Review* (93):7–28.

Cravino, Javier, Daniel Lederman, and Marcelo Olarreaga. 2009. Foreign Direct Investment in Latin America During the Emergence of China and India: Stylized Facts. In *China's and India's Challenge to Latin America: Opportunity or Threat?* ed. D. Lederman, M. Olarreaga, and G. E. Perry. Washington, DC: World Bank.

Cypher, James. 1990. *State and Capital in Mexico: Development Policy Since 1940*. Boulder, CO: Westview Press.

———. 2007. Back to the 19th Century? The Current Commodities Boom and the Primarization Process in Latin America. Presented to the LASA XXVII International Congress Session ECO20, Montreal, Canada September 5–8. Montreal, Canada.

Dedrick, Jason, and Kenneth L. Kraemer. 2002. Enter the Dragon: China's Computer Industry. *Perspectives*, 28–36.

Denae Thrasher, Rachel, and Kevin P. Gallagher. 2008. *21st Century Trade Agreements: Implications for Long-Run Development Policy*. Boston: Frederick Pardee Center for the Study of the Longer-Range Future.

Deutsche Bank Research. 2006. *China's Commodity Hunger: Implications for Africa and Latin America*. Frankfurt: Deutsche Bank.

Devlin, Robert. 2008. China's Economic Rise. In *China's Expansion into the Western Hemisphere: Implications for Latin America and the United States*, ed. R. Roett and G. Paz. Washington, DC: Brookings Institution Press.

Devlin, Robert, Antoni Estevadcordal, and Andres Rodriguez-Clare, eds. 2006. *The Emergence of China: Opportunities and Challenges for Latin America and the Caribbean*. Washington, DC: Inter-American Development Bank; David Rockefeller Center for Latin American Studies, Harvard University.

Domínguez, Jorge I. 2006. *China's Relations with Latin America: Shared Gains, Asymmetric Hopes*. Washington, DC: Inter-American Dialogue.

Dosi, Giovanni, and Luc Soete. 1983. Technology Gaps and Cost-Based Adjustments: Some Explorations on the Determinants of International Competitiveness. *Metroeconomica* 35 (3):197–222.

Dussel Peters, Enrique. 1999. Reflexiones sobre conceptos y experiencias internacionales de industrializacion regional. In *Dinamica Regional y Competitividad Industrial*, ed. Carmen Ruiz Duran and Enrique Dussel Peters. Mexico City: Editorial JUS.

————. 2003. Industrial Policy, Regional Trends, and Structural Change in Mexico's Manufacturing Sector. In *Confronting Development, Assessing Mexico's Economic and Social Policy Challenges*, ed. K. J. Middlebrook and Eduardo Zepeda. Stanford: Stanford University Press.

————. 2004. Gastos en Investigacion y Desarrollo e Inversion Extranjera Directa: Un Estudio a Nivel de Clases Economicas del Sector Manufacturero Mexicano (1994 to 2000). In *Nuevos Caminos Para el Desarollo Sustentable en Mexico*, ed. A. Nadal., Mexico City: El Colegio de Mexico Prensa .

————. 2005. *Economic Opportunities and Challenges Posed by China for Mexico and Central America*. German Development Institute (DIE).

————. 2008a. *Invesion extranjera directa en Mexico: Desempeño y potencial. .* Mexico City: Siglo XXI.

————. 2008b. The Mexico-China Economic Relationship in Electronics: A Case Study of the PC Industry in Jalisco. In *The Impact of China's Global Economic Expansion on Latin America*, ed. R. Jenkins. Norwich, UK: University of East Anglia.

Dussel Peters, Enrique., ed. 2007. *Opportunidades en la relacion economica y commercial entre China y Mexico. Economic Commission for Latin America and the Caribbean* (CEPAL), Santiago, Chile.

Dussel Peters, Enrique, Juan Jose Palacios Lara, and Guillermo Woo Gomez. 2003. *La industria Electronica en Mexico: Problematica, Perspectivas y Propuestas*. Guadalajara: Universidad de Guadalajara.

ECLAC. 1999. *Foreign Direct Investment in Latin America, 1999*. Santiago, Chile: United Nations.

————. 2001. *Economic Survey of Latin America and the Caribbean*. Santiago, Chile: United Nations.

————. 2009. *The Reactions of the Governments of the Americas to the International Crisis: An Overview of Policy Measures up to 31 May 2009*. Santiago, Chile: United Nations.

Economy, Elizabeth. 2004. *The River Runs Black: The Environmental Challenge to China's Future*. Ithaca: Cornell University Press.

Elkan, V. 1996. Catching Up and Slowing Down: Learning and Growth Pattern in an Open Economy. *Journal of International Economy* (41):95–111.

Ellis, Evan R. 2006. The New Chinese Engagement with Latin America. *Air and Space Power Journal* (http://www.airpower.maxwell.af.mil/airchronicles/apje.html).

————. 2008. *China in Latin America*. Boulder: Lynne Rienner.

Fan, P., X. Gao, and C. Watanabe. 2007. Technology Strategies of Innovative Chinese Domestic Companies. *International Journal of Technology and Globalisation* 3 (4):344–363.

Fan, P., and C. Watanabe. 2006. Promoting Industrial Development Through Technology Policy: Lessons from Japan and China. *Technology in Society* 28:303–320.

Federal Reserve Bank of Dallas, ed. 2003. *China: Awakening Giant*. Dallas: Federal Reserve Bank of Dallas.

Feenstra, Robert C., and Hiau Looi Kee. 2007. Trade Liberalisation and Export Variety: A Comparison of Mexico and China. *The World Economy* 30 (1):5–21.

Fernández, J. 2000. The Macroeconomic Setting for Innovation. In *Developing Innovation Systems: Mexico in Global Perspective*, ed. M. Cimoli. New York and London: Continuum Books.

Freund, Caroline. 2009. Effects on Services Trade with the United States. In *China's and India's Challenge to Latin America: Opportunity or Threat?*, ed. D. Lederman, M. Olarreaga, and G. E. Perry. Washington, DC: World Bank.

Freund, Caroline, and Caglar Ozden. 2009. The Effect of China's Exports on Latin American Trade with the World. In *China's and India's Challenge to Latin America: Opportunity or Threat?*, ed. D. Lederman, M. Olarreaga, and G. E. Perry. Washington, DC: World Bank.

Gallagher, Kevin P., Juan Carlos Moreno-Brid, and Roberto Porzecanski. 2008. The Dynamism of Mexican Exports: Lost in (Chinese) Translation? *World Development* 36 (8):1365–1380.

Gallagher, Kevin P., and Roberto Porzecanski. 2007. What a Difference a Few Years Makes: China and the Competitiveness of Mexican Exports. *Oxford Development Studies* 35 (2): 219–223.

———. 2008. *Climbing Up the Technology Ladder? High Technology Exports in China and Latin America*. Berkeley: Center for Latin American Studies, University of California–Berkeley.

Gallagher, Kevin P., and Lyuba Zarsky. 2007. *The Enclave Economy: Investment and Sustainable Development in Mexico's Silicon Valley*. Cambridge, MA: MIT Press.

Gao, G., K. Hin Chai, J. Liu, and J. Li. 2007. Overcoming "'Latecomer Disadvantages'" in Small and Medium-Sized Firms: Evidence from China. *International Journal of Technology and Globalisation* 3 (4):364–383.

Gareffi, Gary, John Humphrey, and Timothy Sturgeon. 2005. The Governance of Global Value Chains. *Review of International Political Economy* 12 (1):78–104.

Girma, S., Y. Gong, and H. Gorg. (2008)., "Foreign Direct Investment, Access to Finance, and Innovation Activity in Chinese enterprises." *World Bank Economic Review*, 22 (2):367–382.

González, Francisco E. 2008. Latin America in the Economic Equation—Winners and Losers: What Can Losers Do? In *China's Expansion in the Western*

Hemisphere: Implications for Latin America and the United States, ed. R. Roett and G. Paz. Washington, DC: Brookings Institution Press.

Görg, H., and David Greenaway. 2004. Much Ado About Nothing? Do Domestic Firms Really Benefit from Foreign Direct Investment. *World Bank Research Observer* 19 (2):171–197.

Gottschalk, Ricardo, and Daniela Prates. 2005. *The Macro-economic Challenges of East Asia's Growing Demand for Primary Commodities in Latin America.* Sussex, UK: Institute for Development Studies.

————. 2006. *East Asia's Growing Demand for Primary Commodities— Macroeconomic Challenges for Latin America.* G-24 Discussion paper. New York: United Nations.

Grossman, Gene, and Elhanan Helpman. 1991. *Innovation and Growth in the Global Economy.* Cambridge: MIT Press.

Gruber, H. 1992. The Learning Curve in the Production of Semiconductor Memory Chips. *Applied Economics* (24):885–894.

Hanson, Gordon H., and Raymond Robertson. 2009. China and the Recent Evolution of Latin America's Manufacturing Exports. In *China's and India's Challenge to Latin America: Opportunity or Threat?*, ed. D. Lederman, M. Olarreaga, and G. E. Perry. Washington, DC: World Bank.

Hausmann, Ricardo, Jason Hwang, and Dani Rodrik. 2005. *What You Export Matters.* Cambridge, MA: National Bureau of Economic Research.

Hogenboom, Barbara. 2009. Latin America and the Rise of China: Possibilities and Obstacles for Development. In *Global Giant: Is China Changing the Rules of the Game?*, ed. E. Paus, P. B. Prime, and J. Western. New York: Palgrave Macmillan.

Imbs, Jean, and Romain Wacziarg. 2003. Stages of Diversification. *American Economic Review* 93 (1):63–86.

Instituto Nacional de Estadística y Geografía de México (INEGI). 2006. www.gob.mx.inegi.

International Monetary Fund. 2006. *World Economic Outlook.* Washington, DC: IMF.

————. 2008. *World Economic Outlook.* Washington, DC: IMF.

————. 2009. *World Economic Outlook.* Washington, DC: IMF.

Jenkins, Rhys. 2008. Measuring the Competitive Threat from China for Other Southern Exporters. *World Economy* 31 (10):1351–1360.

————. 2009. Latin America faces the Chinese Dragon: Opportunities, Challenges and Responses. World Economy and Finance & Economy and Social Research Council Briefing Paper, April. http://www.uea.ac.uk/polopoly_fs/1.113466!ChinaBriefing_8pp.pdf.

————. 2010. The Economic Impacts of China's Global Expansion on Latin America. In *China and Latin America: Economic Relations in the Twenty-first Century*, ed. R. Jenkins and E. Dussel Peters. Bonn: German Development Institute.

Jenkins, Rhys, Enrique Dussel Peters, and Mauricio Mesquita Moreira. 2006. The Impact of China in Latin America and the Caribbean—An Agenda for Research. In *Seventh Annual Global Development Conference, Pre-Conference Workshop on Asian and Other Drivers of Global Change*. St. Petersburg, Russia.

Jianwu, He, Shantong Li, and Sandra Polaski. 2007. *China's Economic Prospects, 2006–2020*. Washington, DC: Carnegie Endowment for International Peace.

Jiménez, Juan Pablo, and Varinia Tromben. 2006. Fiscal Policy and the Commodities Boom: The Impact of Higher Prices for Non-Renewables in Latin America and the Caribbean. *Cepal Review* (90):59–83.

Jones, Ronald W. 1987. Heckscher-Ohlin Trade Theory. In *The New Palgrave: A Dictionary of Economics*, ed. J. Eatwell, M. Milgate, and P. Newman. London: Macmillan.

Kehoe, Timothy J. 1995. A Review of Mexico's Trade Policy from 1982–1994. *The World Economy* (18): 135–151

Krugman, Paul. 1984. Import Protection as Export Promotion: International Competition in the Presence of Oligopoly and Economics of Scale. In *Monopolistic Competition and International Trade*, ed. H. Kierzkowzki. Oxford: Clarendon Press.

Lall, Sanjaya. 1993. Policies for Building Technological Capabilities: Lesson from Asian Experience. *Asian Development Review* 11 (2):72–103.

————. 2000. The Technological Structure and Performance of Developing Country Manufactured Exports, 1985–98. *Oxford Development Studies* 28 (3):337–369.

————. 2005. Rethinking Industrial Strategy: The Role of the State in the Face of Globalization. In *Putting Development First: The Importance of Policy Space in the WTO and IFIs*, ed. K. P. Gallagher. London: Zed Books.

Lall, Sanjaya, and John Weiss. 2005. People's Republic of China's Competitive Threat to Latin America: An Analysis for 1990–2002. *Oxford Development Studies* 33 (2):163–194.

Lall, Sanjaya, John Weiss, and Jinkang Zhang. 2005. *The "Sophistication" of Exports: A New Measure of Product Characteristics*. Manila: Asian Development Bank Institute.

Laursen, Keld. 1998. *Revealed Comparative Advantage and the Alternatives as Measures of International Specialization*. Copenhagen: Danish Research Unit for Industrial Dynamics (DRUIC).

Lazonick, W. 1991. *Business Organization and the Myth of Market Economy.* New York and Melbourne: Cambridge University Press.

Lederman, Daniel, Marcelo Olarreaga, and Guillermo E. Perry. 2009. Latin America's Response to China and India: Overview of Research Findings and Policy Implications. In *China's and India's Challenge to Latin America: Opportunity or Threat?*, ed. D. Lederman, M. Olarreaga, and G. E. Perry. Washington, DC: World Bank, Latin America and the Caribbean Region.

Li, S., and J. Xia. 2008. The Roles and Performance of State Firms and Non-State Firms in China's Economic Transition. *World Development* 36 (1): 39–54.

Linder, S.B. 1961. *An Essay on Trade and Transformation.* New York: John Wiley.

López, Andrés, and Daniela Ramos. 2007. *A Study of the Impact of China's Global Expansion on Argentina.* In *China and Latin America: Economic Relations in the Twenty-first Century*, ed. R. Jenkins and E. Dussel Peters. Bonn: German Development Institute

Lucas, R.E. 1988. On the Mechanics of Economic Development. *Journal of Monetary Economics* 22 (1):3–42.

Lustig, Nora. 1998. *Mexico: The Remaking of an Economy.* Washington, DC: Brookings Institution.

Mattar, J., Juan Carlos Moreno-Brid, and Wilson Peres. 2003. Foreign Investment in Mexico After Economic Reform. In *Confronting Development: Assessing Mexico's Economic and Social Policy Challenges*, ed. K. J. Middlebrook and E. Zepeda. Stanford: Stanford University Press.

Mesquita Moreira, Mauricio. 2004. *Fear of China: Is There a Future for Manufacturing in Latin America?* Washington, DC: Latin America/Caribbean and Asia/Pacific Economics and Business Association.

———. 2007. Fear of China: Is There a Future for Manufacturing in Latin America? *World Development* 35 (3):355–376.

Ministry of Finance (Chile). 2009. *Annual Report: Sovereign Wealth Funds.* Santiago, Chile: Ministry of Finance.

Moore, R. 1997. Learning-by-Doing and Trade Policy in a Developing Economy. *Journal of Developing Areas* (31):515–528.

MOST. 2006. *National High Tech R&D Program (863 Program).* Beijing: Ministry of Science and Technology of the People's Republic of China.

Naugthon, Barry. 2007. *The Chinese Economy: Transitions and Growth.* Cambridge, MA: MIT Press.

Nelson, Richard R., and Sidney G. Winter. 1982. *An Evolutionary Theory of Economic Change.* Cambridge, MA: Harvard University Press.

Ocampo, Jose Antonio. 1993. Terms of Trade and Center-Periphery Relations. In *Development From Within: Toward a Neostructuralist Approach for Latin America*, ed. O. Sunkel. Boulder, CO, and London: Lynne Rienner.

———. 2007. The Macroeconomics of the Latin American Economic Boom. *CEPAL Review* (93):7–28.

———. 2009. Latin America and the Global Financial Crisis. *Cambridge Journal of Economics* 33 (4):703–724.

Ocampo, José Antonio, and María Ángela Parra. 2003. The Terms of Trade for Commodities in the Twentieth Century. *CEPAL Review* (79):7–35.

OECD and FAO. 2009. *OECD-FAO Agricultural Outlook 2009* Paris: OECD.

Otero, Gerardo. 1996. Neoliberal Reform and Politics in Mexico. In *Neoliberalism Revisited: Economic Restructuring and Mexico's Political Future,* ed. G. Otero. Boulder, CO: Westview.

Palacios, Juan. 2001. *Production Networks and Industrial Clustering in Developing Regions: Electronics Manufacturing in Guadalajara, Mexico.* Guadalajara: University of Guadalajara.

Palma, Christian, and Patricio Ojeda. 2009. Gobierno enfrenta la crisis con plan de US$4 mil millones. *La Nación (Chile),* January 6.

Paus, Eva. 2005. *Foreign Direct Investment, Development and Globalization: Can Costa Rica Become Ireland?* London: Palgrave.

———. 2009. The Rise of China: Implications for Latin American Development. *Development Policy Review* 27 (4):419–456.

People's Republic of China. 2006. *Statistical Yearbook.* Beijing.

Phillips, Nicola. 2007. *Consequences of an Emerging China: Is Development Space Disappearing for Latin America and the Caribbean?* Waterloo, UK: Centre for International Governance Innovation.

Pizarro, J., and Mehdi Shafaeddin. 2007. From Export Promotion to Import Substitution: Comparative Experience of China and Mexico, unpublished manuscript.

Prébisch, Raúl. 1951. *Growth, Disequilibrium and Disparities: Interpretation of the Process of Economic Development* (Economic Survey of Latin America 1949). Santiago, Chile: ECLAC.

Puyana, Alicia, and José Romero. 2006. Trade Liberalization in Mexico: Some Macroeconomic and Sectoral Impacts and Implications for Macroeconomic Policy. Paper read at International Development Association (IDEAS) and UNDP Conference on Post Liberalization Constraints on Macroeconomic Policies, January 27–29, at Muttukadu, Chennai.

Qian, Yingyi (with Jinglian Wu). 2003. China's Transition to a Market Economy: How Far Across the River? In *Chinese Policy Reform at the Millennium,* ed. N. C. Hope, D. Tao Yang, and M. Yang Li. Stanford: Stanford University Press.

Ramírez, M. 1994. Public and Private Investment in Mexico, 1950–1990: An Empirical Analysis. *Southern Economic Journal* 61 (1):1–17.

Redding, Stephen. 1999. Dynamic Comparative Advantage and the Welfare Effects of Trade. *Oxford Economic Papers* (51):15–39.

Reynolds, Clark W. 1970. *The Mexican Economy*. New Haven, CT: Yale University Press.

Rivera Vargas, Maria Isabel. 2002. *Technology Transfer via the University-Industry Relationship: The Case of Foreign High Technology Electronics Industry in Mexico's Silicon Valley*. London: Routledge.

Rodrik, Dani. 1999. *The New Global Economy and Developing Countries: Making Openness Work*. Washington, DC: Overseas Development Council.

———. 2005. Policies for Economic Diversification. *CEPAL Review* (87):7–23.

———. 2006. What's So Special About China's Exports? *China & World Economy* 14 (5):1–19.

———. 2007. *One Economics, Many Recipes: Globalization, Institutions, and Economic Growth*. Princeton: Princeton University Press.

Romer, P.M. 1986. Increasing Returns and Long-Run Growth. *Journal of Political Economy* 94 (5):1002–1037.

———. 1987. Growth Based on Increasing Returns Due to Specialization. *American Economic Review, Papers and Proceedings,* 72:52–62.

Romero, Simon, and Alexei Barrionuevo. 2009. Deals Help China Expand Sway in Latin America. *New York Times*, April 15, http://www.nytimes.com/2009/04/16/world/16chinaloan.html.

Romo Murillo, David. 2002. Derramas Tecnologicas de la Inversion Extranhera en la Industria Mexicana. *Comercio Exterior* 53 (3):230–243.

Sachs, Jeffrey, and Andrew Warner. 1995. *Natural Resource Abundance and Economic Growth*. Cambridge, MA: National Bureau of Economic Research.

Sargent, John, and Linda Matthews. 2007. China vs. Mexico in the Global EPZ Industry: Maquiladoras, FDI Quality, and Plant Mortality. Edinburg: University of Texas Pan American Center for Border Economic Studies.

———. 2008. Capital Intensity, Technology Intensity, and Skill Development in Post China/WTO Maquiladoras. *World Development* 36 (4):541–559.

———. 2009. China vs. Mexico in the Global EPZ Industry: Maquiladoras, FDI Quality, and Plant Mortality. *World Development* 37 (6):1069–1082.

Schmitz, H., and T. Hewitt. 1991. Learning to Raise Infants: A Case Study in Industrial Policy. In *States or Markets? Neo-liberalism and the Development Policy Debate*, ed. C. Colclough and J. Manor. Oxford: Clarendon Press.

Shafaeddin, Mehdi. 2005a. Friedrich List and the Infant Industry Argument. In *The Pioneers of Development Economics: Great Economists on Development*, ed. K. S. Jomo. London and New York: Zed Books.

———. 2005b. Towards an Alternative Perspective on Trade and Industrial Policies. *Development and Change* 36 (6):1143–1162.

———. 2005c. *Trade Policy at the Crossroads: Recent Experience of Developing Countries*. New York: Palgrave Macmillan.

Shafaeddin, Mehdi, and Juan Pizarro. 2007. *From Export Promotion to Import Substitution: Comparative Experience of China and Mexico*. Munich: University Library of Munich, Germany.

Singh, A. 1993. *The Plan, the Market and Evolutionary Economic Reform in China*. Geneva: UNCTAD.

Spooner, John G. 2005. *The Nouveau Lenovo Wants to Shake Up the PC Market's Status Quo*. ZDnet [accessed March 3]. Available at www.zdnet.com.

Stimulating: Cashing in the Fruits of Rigour. 2009. *Economist*, February 19. *Available at www.economist.com.*

Teubal, M. 1996. R&D and Technology Policy in NICs as Learning Processes. *World Development* 24 (3):449–460.

UNCTAD. 2008. *World Investment Report*. Geneva: United Nations.

———. 2009. *Handbook of Statistics, 2008*. Geneva: United Nations.

UNCTC. 1992. *Foreign Direct Investment and Industrial Restructuring in Mexico*. New York: United Nations Center on Transnational Corporations.

Unger, K., and M. Oloriz. 2000. Globalization of Production and Technology. In *Developing Innovation Systems: Mexico in Global Perspective*, ed. M. Cimoli. New York and London: Continuum Books.

UNIDO. 1997. *Industrial Development: Global Report 1997*. Oxford: Oxford University Press.

United Nations Statistics Division. 2008. *United Nations Commodity Trade Statistics Database, http://comtrade.un.org,* COMTRADE.

———. 2009. *United Nations Commodity Trade Statistics Database (COMTRADE)*.

USDA Economic Research Service. 2009. *International Macroeconomic Data Set: Real Exchange Rates Historica.*, Washington, DC: U.S. Department of Agriculture.

USDOC. 2006. *Technology Transfer to China*, ed. Bureau of Industry and Security Washington, DC: U.S. Department of Commerce.

Vera-Diaz, Maria, Robert K. Kaufmann, Daniel Neptstad, and Peter Schlesinger. 2008. An Interdisciplinary Model of Soybean Yield in the Amazon Basin: The Climatic, Edaphic, and Economic Determinants. *Ecological Economics* 65 (2):420–431.

Walsh, K. 2003. Foreign High-Tech R&D in China: Risks, Rewards, and Implications for US-China Relations. Washington, D.C.: Henry L. Stimson Centre.

Wang, Q., and H. Wang. 2007. Industrial Standard Based Competition and Chinese Firm Strategic Choice. *International Journal of Globalisation* 3 (4):422–436.

Wise, Carol, ed. 1998. *The Post-NAFTA Political Economy: Mexico and the Western Hemisphere*. University Park: Pennsylvania State University Press.

Wise, Carol, and Cintia Quiliconi. 2007. China's Surge in Latin American Markets: Policy Challenges and Responses. *Politics & Policy* 35 (3):410–438.

World Bank. 2008. *World Development Indicators*. Washington, DC: World Bank.

———. 2009. *World Development Indicators*. Washington, DC: World Bank.

Wray, W. 2008. The Commodities Market Bubble. *Public Policy Brief*: Annandale-on-Hudson, NY: Levy Economics Institute of Bard College.

Xiwei, Z., and Y. Xiangdong. 2007. Science and Technology Policy Reform and Its Impact on China's National Innovation System. *Technology and Science* (29):317–325.

Ye, Min. 2008. Developmental State—China's Government's Role in China's Electronics Industry. *The Waseda Journal of Political Science and Economics*. 356(67).

About the Authors

Kevin P. Gallagher is an associate professor in the Department of International Relations at Boston University and senior researcher at the Global Development and Environment Institute at Tufts University. He specializes in global economic and development policy, with an emphasis on Latin America. Professor Gallagher is the author of *The Enclave Economy: Foreign Investment and Sustainable Development in Mexico's Silicon Valley* (with Lyuba Zarsky), and *Free Trade and the Environment: Mexico, NAFTA, and Beyond.* He has been the editor or co-editor of a number of books, including *Rethinking Foreign Investment for Sustainable Development: Lessons from Latin America,* and *Putting Development First: The Importance of Policy Space in the WTO and IFIs.* He writes a monthly column on globalization and development for the *Guardian* (UK) newspaper. Professor Gallagher is also a research fellow at Boston University's Frederick S. Pardee Center for the Study of the Longer-Range Future, where he directs the Global Economic Governance Initiative.

Roberto Porzecanski received his BA in international studies from Universidad ORT Uruguay (2001), a Diploma in Economics from Uruguay's Universidad de la República (2003), and his Master of Arts in law and diplomacy from the Fletcher School of Law and Diplomacy, at Tufts University in 2005. In 2010, he got his PhD in international relations, also from the Fletcher School. Between 2005 and 2010 he was a researcher at the Global Development and Environment Institute, also at Tufts. He specializes in global economic policy, with an emphasis on the political economy of trade liberalization in Latin America. He is the author of *No voy en tren: Uruguay y las perspectivas de un TLC con Estados Unidos (2000–2010)*, published earlier this year by Debate (Random House Mondadori) in Uruguay, and of numerous articles in peer-reviewed journals. Since 2004, Roberto Porzecanski has also been the U.S. correspondent for Radio El Espectador, the leading Uruguayan news radio station.

Index